JOSEPH

'Meg Warner moves us on from Lloyd Webber's 'Poor, poor Joseph' to meet a man trafficked and traumatised, by no means perfect, but for us a lesson in building resilience. Tracing her own story, which includes being limited by illness and finding work in a new country, Warner draws on biblical scholarship and research into trauma and resilience.

'This book is written in both a down to earth and intelligent way, so that we weave our story, the author's and Joseph's with contemporary issues, and consider how we have come through difficulties and can become more resilient in the future.'
Justine Allain Chapman, Archdeacon of Boston, England, and author of *The Resilient Disciple*

'Meg Warner brings together a depth of biblical knowledge and a strong understanding of contemporary research on the impact of trauma on individuals and communities in her exploration of the story of the well-known biblical character of Joseph. She invites her readers into a deeper understanding of the way that the trauma of the ancient Israelite community is reflected in the Bible, and shows how this story continues to resonate with our own experiences of pain and suffering.

'Along the way she shares her own story and invites us into a reflection of our own experiences, taking her reader on a journey of exploration without falling into the trap of prescribing the outcome. The book is carefully written and astute, full of compassion, hope and sensitivity. A great read for individuals wanting to explore issues of trauma and its impact, this book is also an invaluable resource for groups.'
Liz Boase, Dean of the School of Graduate Research, University of Divinity, Australia, and co-editor of *Bible Through the Lens of Trauma*

'This book is electric. Meg Warner has that rare knack of using personal story to bring the biblical story to life. At every step she draws us in, challenging us to allow the biblical story, in turn, to bring us to life. It makes for compulsive reading.'
Nicholas Holtam, Bishop of Salisbury

'With characteristic deftness, disarming honesty and exegetical skill, Meg Warner makes the story of Joseph a parable for our lives and our times.'
Sam Wells, Vicar of St Martin-in-the-Fields, Trafalgar Square, London

JOSEPH

A story of resilience

Meg Warner

First published in Great Britain in 2020

Society for Promoting Christian Knowledge
36 Causton Street
London SW1P 4ST
www.spck.org.uk

British Library Cataloguing-in-Publication Data
A catalogue record for this book is available from the British Library

ISBN 978–0–281–08108–0
eBook ISBN 978–0–281–08109–7

Typeset by Nord Compo
First printed in Great Britain by Jellyfish Print Solutions
Subsequently digitally printed in Great Britain

eBook by Nord Compo

Produced on paper from sustainable forests

Meg Warner is Tutor in Old Testament at Northern College, Manchester. She is a Reader in the Church of England, a regular guest speaker at synods, festivals and other church gatherings around the UK and internationally, and (writing as Megan Warner) author and editor of several books, most recently *Re-Imagining Abraham: A Re-Assessment of the Influence of Deuteronomism in Genesis* (Brill, 2018), *Confronting Religious Violence: A Counter-Narrative* (with Richard A. Burridge and Jonathan Sacks, Baylor, 2018) and *Tragedies and Christian Congregations: The Practical Theology of Trauma* (Routledge, 2020). *Joseph: A story of resilience* is the follow-up to her highly successful Lent book, *Abraham: A journey through Lent* (SPCK, 2015).

For Christopher Southgate, Hilary Ison and Carla Grosch-Miller, with thanks for recruiting me, and then being recruited in return.

And for Ian Markham. He knows why.

Contents

Contents

Contents

Acknowledgements

One of the ways of being resilient through a crisis, I've discovered, is to write a book about it. Having this book already in the pipeline has been, quite literally, a godsend at one of the most challenging times of my life.

Thank you to Philip Law and his fabulous team at SPCK for continuing to believe in me and for being patient when it all started to take just a little longer than originally planned.

I'd also like to thank the Templeton World Charities Trust. Although this book is not one of their sponsored projects, it would never have come about without their support of the 'Tragedies and Congregations Project', based at the University of Exeter and led by the amazing Christopher Southgate. It was on this project that I learned about trauma and found myself being edged, just in time, towards an interest in resilience. Chris, Hilary and Carla were the best colleagues in that project that I could possibly have hoped for, and I owe all three of them a great deal.

Once again, I want to express my thanks to the staff and students of Virginia Theological Seminary and especially Ian and Lesley Markham. They don't all know that they're lifesavers, but they are.

Many people have been praying for and being friends to R. and me while I have been writing this book, and I am thankful for every one of them. Some of them have been Polly and Adrian, Sarah and Carl, John-Francis, Nigel and Stephen, the gals of SNOG, Judi, Martin, Susannah, Justin, Gordon, Rowan, Nick, Gilly and Dunc, Jonathan, Steve, Ed, John and Jenny. There have been others. Thank you; you got us through.

Others have been influential during various stages of writing this book, and I'd like to thank all those at St Luke's West Holloway who signed up to come to my 'Joseph' Lent group, as well as the members of my Oxford Summer School class in August 2019, for highly stimulating and challenging conversation.

So I think that just leaves R., without whom this book would have got to the publishers on time. But without whom there wouldn't have been a book. Shalom, my love.

A Note from the Author

Books tend, by their nature, to be written at particular times and in particular contexts. Because the writing, editing, proofing and production stages of books happen across extended periods, the contexts in which they are finally published can be markedly different from those pertaining during the writing phase. That is the case for *Joseph: A story of resilience*. While I was writing the original drafts, years ago now, Brexit was still a pipe dream and none of us imagined the political landscape that we now see all around us. Later, in the editing stages, Brexit happened, and I was able to refer to it along the way. Brexit seemed, then, to be the greatest challenge to have struck the UK for many decades. Today, however, as this book enters its final stages of publication, the UK has very suddenly been hit by the realities of the Coronavirus pandemic, and they threaten to overshadow Brexit dramatically.

There are many, many new things, and fears, to get our individual and collective heads around. One of the strangest is the idea that the way we can best support and care for one another is to keep our distance. That idea goes against everything we have been conditioned to believe. We are, however, going to have to 're-frame' much of what we have been conditioned to believe, or to assume, in the wake of this virus. (I talk about the process of 're-framing' in Chapter Three.)

I cannot know in what kind of context you will find yourself when you pick up this book. You may still be in the grip of the Corona crisis, or you may be gratefully out the other end, and enjoying, once again, all sorts of things that you used to take for granted: visiting friends, going out for a meal, shopping, attending work or school, and buying toilet paper without feeling a rush of guilty achievement…

What I do know is that the pressure on every single one of us – individuals and communities alike – to be resilient and to practise resilience will have grown exponentially. Some of us will have faced, or cheated, death, lost friends and loved ones, or become profoundly and irretrievably isolated. All of us will find ourselves living in a new world, in which the things we always thought we could rely on could be taken away from us very suddenly, and where even wealth and privilege cannot keep us safe and well. The need for theological reflection about resilience, especially in conversation with Scripture, will also continue to grow. I hope that this book might be a resource that speaks to you in your context, whatever that might be, and that helps you to find God there with you.

Shalom

Meg
Manchester
20 March, 2020

1

The dreamer

GENESIS 37

Dear Dr Warner, ...
... we regret to inform you ...
... a surprisingly strong field ...
... best wishes for your job search ...

I sighed as I added the latest rejection letter to the growing pile. In my innocence I had imagined the field of Old Testament Studies to be small and rarefied in my adopted homeland. Nothing could be further from the truth! The United Kingdom, it appears, is awash with academics determined to spend their careers arguing about variant traditions in the book of Esther and teaching Baruch to spotty undergraduates. And they are all currently looking for jobs, and they are all prepared to commute from Land's End to northern Scotland to do them.

I moved to London from Melbourne, Australia, five years ago to get married, and I have been applying for jobs here ever since. You know, I've always rather loved those books where the heroine meets a ridiculously charming foreigner, romantically tosses her life in to travel to his country and marry him, and then caps off the whole adventure by writing a book about it. I've enjoyed reading those kinds of books, but it never in my wildest dreams occurred to me that one day I might actually write one. Nevertheless, that's exactly what I did. In my previous book, *Abraham: A journey through Lent*, I told the story of meeting my now husband (I called him 'R.'), leaving my home and job and family in Australia and travelling to the

1

UK. I told it alongside the story of Abraham's journey from Ur in the Chaldeans, via Haran, to the land that God promised to give him and his family in Canaan. Along the way, I encouraged readers just like you to tell the stories of your own lives, too, alongside Abraham's story.

In this book, my plan is to pick up my story where I left off – after the honeymoon ends – and, taking Joseph (the 'Technicolor Dreamcoat' one) as my companion, to tell the story of the next part of the journey – including the job applications! You don't need to have read *Abraham: A journey* in order to read and enjoy this book, but I will refer to it from time to time, just as I will refer from time to time to Abraham himself. Indeed, one of the things I have learned over these last years is that what happens at the beginning of a story plays an awfully big role in what happens later on.

Why 'resilience'?

Have you ever had to struggle to find a job, as I've been doing lately? There are several reasons why being unemployed is a challenging experience. I'm fortunate enough to have married a husband who has supported me while I've been looking for work, so that I haven't had to worry about the most pressing challenges of finding food and shelter. I've also picked up bits and pieces of teaching from time to time, and I've had plenty of writing to keep me occupied. Even so, I've found that being more or less unemployed has been difficult in all sorts of ways. Especially in a new country, it is isolating to be without a work community and to lack work-based avenues for meeting new people and becoming acquainted with the professional 'scene'. But perhaps the most challenging aspect has been the actual process of applying for jobs. As you may also have discovered for yourself, every time you write a new application, you have to become emotionally attached, to some degree, to the job you're applying for. You have to imagine yourself into the new job – try it on for size in your mind – and generate some excitement about the new life you would have if you were to be successful and get it. Your application must say that *this* is the job that I really want (and would be perfect for), not *this* or *that* other job, and in order to say so convincingly, whether in your application letter or in person in an interview, you must actually come to believe it. Each time you apply for a new job, you have to prepare yourself for the emotional rollercoaster that is inevitably coming, being willing to allow yourself to get excited about what this potential new life might be like, while at the same time preparing yourself for the likelihood that you will be unsuccessful and that your potential new employer will not only reject you, but also cut off the glossy new future that you've hesitantly (or wholeheartedly!) allowed yourself to believe in.

I've been trying to decide whether I think that, if I'm not going to get a particular job, it is better to be short-listed or just rejected immediately. It's a bit six of one and half-dozen of the other. Not being short-listed can be a real blow. But while being offered an interview is a great boost to the morale, it means travelling further along the emotional trajectory I've just described, and the eventual rejection can feel all the more devastating when it comes from somebody in front of whom you've made yourself vulnerable at interview. Short-listed or not, applying for a series of jobs like this over a long period of time requires one to have some internal reserves. You need to be able to withstand repeated rejection and to find a way of resigning yourself to the loss of a procession of bright, shiny new futures.

I've now spent six years in London looking for work. Various smaller things have come along, but not *the* job I've been looking for, despite the fact that I've made any number of applications and turned up for a succession of interviews. It is strangely disconcerting. In my Australian life, I'd only officially applied for jobs twice. The first application, at the end of my law degree, led to five job offers, and I had the luxury of choosing between them. Later, when ill health meant that I couldn't practice law any longer, I applied for and got a teaching job in the law school where I'd studied. After that, jobs seemed to come and apply for me rather than the other way round! The opportunities I needed had an extraordinary way of turning up just exactly at the moment I needed them, even when my health was at its worst. It became part of my self-understanding of who I was as a child of God that the next thing would come and present itself when it was needed. On the other hand, I was absolutely rubbish at romantic relationships. I simply couldn't put a foot right. Now the tables are turned – I have a husband, and I can't get a job! What has happened, *and who am I*?

Of course, things could be far, far worse. I could have been kidnapped by my siblings, trafficked into slavery and then sexually abused like our hero Joseph. Finding it difficult to secure a full-time job is one thing, but Joseph's story begins with a full-scale disaster, as the patience of his 11 brothers with their frankly objectionable sibling finally gives out, and they sell him to some passing traders en route to Egypt.

The two scenarios I've drawn – on the one hand, my protracted search for validation through employment, and, on the other, the acute trauma of betrayal and loss of personal freedom, agency and homeland suffered by Joseph – are illustrative of different kinds of personal challenges. One kind involves coping with an extended experience of difficult or testing circumstances. The other involves surviving a major disaster and then finding a way to come to terms with its impact. Each of these kinds of challenges can be stressful, or traumatic, in its own way, and both make demands on those who experience them. One of the great conundrums of our time is why some people seem to handle, or recover from, such experiences relatively well, even perhaps seeming to blossom or grow in the face of the challenge, while others are knocked about or even defeated by the same set of circumstances. The trait, or skill, exhibited by those who cope well with challenging circumstances is called 'resilience'. There has been a huge amount of research done into resilience in recent years, and nearly all of it suggests that resilience isn't just something you're born with, but is something you can learn and develop.

'Resilience' has become a buzzword in recent years. If you start looking out for it, you soon find yourself seeing it everywhere. Everybody wants to discover how to build their resilience and how to be more resilient than the next person. Indeed, resilience has become a bit faddish. And like every fad, it has its dark side as well as its benefits. One of the 'fads' that preceded resilience, you might remember, was 'mindfulness'. Both resilience and mindfulness are enormously valuable in and of themselves, and even though both may sound very 'twenty-first century', they both have origins in Christian tradition and in the traditions of other ancient religions. But in the wrong hands, each can be used as an abusive weapon instead of a supportive tool. Let me give you an example: as mindfulness training started to proliferate in the corporate world, people began to suspect that corporate bosses had more than the simple well-being of their employees in mind. Did they really just want to improve the lives of their often stressed or exhausted employees, or was their primary concern to equip those same employees to work even longer hours, being even more productive? In a similar way, a danger of the increased interest in resilience is that resilience becomes just another 'skill' that is measured and weighed and demanded of people, so that those who do not cope can be criticized for lacking it, while ideals of resilience can be used by the powerful as reasons for withholding fair treatment or justice from the more vulnerable.

Earlier this year, I read a disturbing news story. A Syrian refugee couple and their two daughters, who fled Syria and came to the UK in 2012, appealed to their local council for help after they had been evicted (through no fault of their own) from their privately rented home. The council refused to help, saying that the family was 'resilient enough' to cope with the experience of homelessness. Now, I can't comment on the rightness or wrongness of the council's decision not to help, but the idea that any family, let alone a refugee family, might justifiably be expected to possess sufficient levels of resilience to sail through an experience of homelessness seems extraordinary! It also seems just a little bit abusive.

This is going to be a book about learning and developing resilience. But it will also be one in which I will encourage you to think about some of the darker aspects of our society's current fixation on resilience. Whom does resilience benefit, whom may it harm, and where does it sit in a life of faith? It will also be a book about stories. I'll tell you the story of what has happened to me since I set out on my Awfully Big Adventure to live in London, and especially the bits of it that have required resilience. I'll also encourage you to think about some of your stories and the role resilience plays in your life and how you might think about building it up. Along the way, I'm going to tell the story of Joseph. It could be thought of as the *quintessential* resilience story, in which the younger son who is hated by his brothers and sold by them into slavery flourishes so that he becomes the second most powerful man in Egypt and his childhood dreams of his family bowing down to him all come true.

No story is ever quite what it seems on the surface, though, is it? Is the story of Joseph one for us to emulate, or is it a cautionary tale? Or a bit of both? Let's get started and find out.

Meeting Joseph

Then Judah said to his brothers, 'What profit is it if we kill our brother and conceal his blood? Come, let us sell him to the Ishmaelites, and not lay our hands on him, for he is our brother, our own flesh.' And his brothers agreed. When some Midianite traders passed by, they drew Joseph up, lifting him out of the pit, and sold him to the Ishmaelites for twenty pieces of silver. And they took Joseph to Egypt. (Gen. 37.26–28)

How well do you know the story of Joseph? Is it one of your favourites? Do you perhaps know the Andrew Lloyd-Webber/Tim Rice version better than you know the Genesis original? When I worked with the Joseph story with a group from my church, we discovered that many of us know the musical better than the biblical story, and that we found it difficult to read Genesis without images from the stage show dominating our imagination. Partly as a result of this influence, but also partly as a result of the way the story has traditionally been read, Joseph has occupied a position quite like that of Abraham in our imaginations. If Abraham is thought of as a towering figure of faith, then Joseph is seen as a model of wisdom and righteousness. Joseph is the character who overcomes all manner of adversities, who is blessed with special foreknowledge and understanding from God and who uses his gifts to save a foreign nation as well as the brothers who so cruelly betrayed him at the beginning of the story. If you've read *Abraham: A journey*, you'll know that Abraham is a far more complex and compromised character than we sometimes acknowledge. Will something similar prove to be true of Joseph?

Joseph's story begins in Chapter 37 of Genesis. We learn that Joseph's father, Jacob, settles with his family in the land of Canaan – the land that God gave to Abraham, and where Abraham and his son, Isaac, Jacob's father, had lived as aliens. Now, Jacob's family is large and unconventional (in another context we'd probably call it 'unbiblical') – he has twelve sons and apparently a number of daughters (although only one, Dinah, is named) by four mothers. Reuben (Jacob's firstborn), Simeon, Levi, Judah, Isachar, Zebulun and Dinah are the children of Jacob's first wife, Leah, while Gad and Asher are the children of Leah's maid, Zilpah. Joseph and Benjamin, the two youngest, are the sons of Jacob's second wife, Leah's sister Rachel, while Dan and Naphtali are the children of Rachel's maid, Bilhah. Confused? Good – you should be!

'This is the story of the family of Jacob,' says Genesis 37.2. But right from the very next verse, most of the attention in the story is directed toward Joseph, Jacob's second-youngest son. Whose story is this going to be? We typically call Genesis 37–50 the 'Joseph story' or 'saga', but it is true that the story is also about Joseph's father and brothers – and at certain points, some of them are going to prove to be almost as important as Joseph.

Apparently, the young Joseph was a thoroughly objectionable character; I have a great deal of sympathy with his brothers! Joseph was a snitch who used to tell tales about his brothers to their father. He was also his father's favourite, and to be honest, Jacob seems to have been part of the problem. Jacob unwisely displayed his favouritism openly, sending Joseph out to spy on his brothers and marking him out by the gift of a special robe. To make matters worse, Joseph was foolish enough to tell his brothers about his dreams in which his family would bow down before him. Joseph's brothers were understandably jealous and resentful of Joseph. They hated him.

The story goes on to tell about how Joseph's brothers sell him into slavery, but it might be worth pausing at this point to recognize that, as bad as Joseph's experience is about to become, his childhood could not have been easy. Undoubtedly, he had an inflated view of his own importance (whether that view was justified is one of the central questions of the story), but even so, the text suggests that, as a youth, he experienced antagonism and ostracism from his brothers and sisters. As much as I sympathize with them, my experience of being bullied at school does give me a degree of sympathy for Joseph also. He receives signs of his own specialness in his dreams and in the favouritism of his father, but he is not sufficiently socially aware to be able to navigate life with his siblings in a way that wins from them anything but jealousy, resentment and hatred.

I'm glad to be able to report that I was never tempted to tell my family or my schoolmates that they would one day bow down before me. Nevertheless, I was brighter than many of my classmates in the small country town where I grew up, and I was keen to work hard and do well. Like Joseph, however, I lacked the social intelligence that might have cautioned me to hide or modify some of the things about me that made me different from my classmates – so they bullied me. Even, I'm afraid, some of the teachers bullied me! Looking back, I can see how I might have been insufferable, but that schoolyard treatment had an impact, and I learned to see the world as a threatening and potentially dangerous place. I look at children and young adults today and wonder how they cope in a world in which students take 'the playground' home with them at the end of the school day through social media – and where popularity and self-worth are measured through numbers of online 'friends' or 'followers' and where the anonymity of the screen encourages casual cruelty. I might not have survived such a world, because my coping mechanisms weren't very good. I tended not to tell anyone when major instances of bullying occurred, because I was too embarrassed. I also didn't really know how to modulate my behaviour effectively, so I mostly just kept on going and trying harder, in the hope that people would eventually decide I was all right. I was finally saved when my mother happened to witness me being bullied by one of my teachers. As soon as they could, my parents arranged for me to go to a boarding school in a bigger town. At least I wasn't bundled off to the highest bidder and taken away by camel train – but, like Joseph, I was sent away.

Did you have your own experiences of bullying when you were younger, or do you have concerns now for your children? If you were bullied at school, what kind of coping mechanisms did you develop? Did they work? How have your experiences in the schoolyard impacted on your adult character and your way of looking at the world? Is the world, for you, a safe place in which you move from one appealing opportunity to the next, or is it a more threatening place where any interaction with other people has the potential to hurt you or undermine your self-confidence? These early experiences can have quite an influence on how we respond to challenges in later life. You may, of course, have experienced serious abuse as a child, whether sexual or some other kind. If that is the case, you will not need me to tell you that those earlier experiences have impacted your way of being an adult in the world – and I hope that you have been able to access the necessary help and support.

The effects of trauma

People respond to traumatic events or circumstances in their lives differently. Modern trauma theory has been developed out of research into the effects of war on returned service personnel and the effects of sexual abuse on children. In both cases, it is possible for individuals to make the transition to ordinary domestic adult life without too many serious consequences, but equally in both cases, such experiences can have an enormous impact on the ability of the individual to adapt – and some never manage to adapt.

I should stress that being affected by trauma is nothing to be ashamed about, and that it is something over which an individual has absolutely no control. It is simply the case that individuals are affected differently. In fact, the effects of trauma are readily recognizable as the body's automatic self-protection systems coming into play. In a situation of trauma, when a person is overwhelmed, the body's automatic reaction is to go into 'fight or flight' mode and either to prepare to run away or to defend itself. When that happens, certain parts of the nervous system go on high alert, while other parts of the body effectively close down. There is little need for complicated speech or thought or for digestion or temperature regulation while the body is under attack, so the parts of the body responsible for those activities close down temporarily, while in other parts of the body, the blood starts to pump and adrenalin to flow.

For some people, with particular experiences of being overwhelmed in the past, the automatic response will be neither 'fight' nor 'flight', but 'freeze'. This is what an animal does when it 'plays dead'. Essentially, most or all of the body's functions close down, and the person stays rooted to the spot. The freeze response may be accompanied by dissociation. When this occurs, the traumatized person may be aware of the overwhelming event happening, but of watching it from some distance away. So, for example, a child who experiences regular sexual abuse may 'watch' herself being abused from the other side of the room or from a position on the ceiling. Just like the 'fight or flight' response, 'freeze' and 'dissociation' are natural ways in which our bodies act to protect us from a situation which threatens to overwhelm us.

All of these bodily responses are normal and helpful, because they allow the body to cope with the 'overwhelm' of the senses that a person experiences in the moment of traumatic injury. The long-term problems arise when, for some reason, the body doesn't or isn't able to return to normal – to re-associate or turn off the fight or flight response and re-engage normal bodily functions of speech and thought, etc. The person who is stuck in 'fight or flight' moves into a kind of functionality in which basic day to day motor functions occur more or less automatically, but in which higher functions of thought and movement are impaired. Because of a tendency to disassociate in 'fight or flight' as well as in 'freeze', it is often difficult for such a person to remember or tell the story of the traumatic event. The person impacted by the traumatic event very often has no real memory of it, because the event was never truly experienced. Instead of remembering, the body stores – and from time to time throws up – shreds of recollection as flashbacks. These can be terrifying. This is particularly so because one of the effects of trauma is that it 'collapses' time, so that it seems to the person having flashbacks that the events being 'replayed' are not stored safely in the past, but happening in the present. Thus, a traumatized person can experience the traumatic event over and over again, while any attempt to describe it may resemble a confused collection of impressions rather than a coherent narrative.

'Um, it was the Ishmaelites – no, wait, it was the Midianites …'

There is a marvellous scene in the very first episode of the BBC sitcom *Rev*. The Reverend Adam Smallbone needs to find a way to choose among the large number of parents who want to have their children admitted to the parish school. He suggests a Bible test and sets up a role play in which his Reader, Nigel, takes on the role of prospective parent, while Adam himself administers the test (with the aid of a ridiculously bright desk light). Nigel, who the viewer soon discovers is almost as great a trial to his vicar as Joseph was to his brothers, accepts the role with relish, but complains that the questions are far too easy. Eventually, once Nigel has responded to the half-question 'Where, today, would you find …?' with the correct answer 'Modern-day Iraq', Adam fires off a trick question: 'Who sold Joseph into captivity?' Nigel is initially stumped, but eventually replies confidently, 'The Midianites'. 'No, it wasn't,' trumpets Adam. 'It was the Ishmaelites.' 'I think you'll find it wasn't,' responds Nigel, somewhat less confidently, and they both have to get out their Bibles. Nigel is right to doubt himself on this one – I have my Bible open in front of me right now, and I honestly can't say whether it was the Ishmaelites or Midianites who sold Joseph into slavery.

Let's back up a bit, and remember the story to that point. On one of the occasions when Jacob sends Joseph out to spy on his brothers, his brothers see him approaching. 'Here comes that dreamer,' they say, and they cook up a plan to kill him. Reuben, the eldest, seems to sense a personal opportunity. He counsels his brothers against killing Joseph and suggests they simply throw him into a pit in the wilderness and leave him there. Reuben secretly wants to curry favour with his father by being the one to restore Joseph to him. In any event, the brothers agree – they strip Joseph of the offending robe, throw him into an empty cistern and settle down to enjoy their lunch. Before too long they spot a group of *Ishmaelite* traders headed south toward Egypt. This time it is Judah who speaks up:

'What profit is it if we kill our brother and conceal his blood? Come, let us sell him to the Ishmaelites and not lay our hands on him, for he is our brother, our own flesh.' His brothers agree. Well, I guess that is one kind of brotherly love! However, according to Genesis 37.28, some *Midianites* then pass by, pull Joseph out of the cistern, and for twenty pieces of silver, sell him to the *Ishmaelite* traders, who take Joseph down to Egypt. In the next verse, it appears that the brothers have been too focused on their lunch to notice any of this. Reuben returns to the cistern, presumably to carry out his earlier plan, and discovers that Joseph is missing. He tears his clothes and returns to tell his brothers the news that Joseph is gone. The brothers slaughter a goat and soil Joseph's distinctive robe with its blood; then they take it to show their father, Jacob. Jacob quickly recognizes the robe and jumps to his own conclusions about the facts of Joseph's demise, from which his sons do not disillusion him. He tears his clothes, puts on sackcloth and mourns his dead son 'for many days', refusing any comfort from his sons or from 'all his [unnamed] daughters'. In the very last verse of the chapter, the reader is told that the *Midianites* had sold Joseph in Egypt to Potiphar, one of Pharaoh's officials and the captain of the guard. No wonder Nigel was confused.

Well, however obnoxious Joseph was, he can't have deserved to have been stripped naked, thrown into a cistern, traded between random sets of pirates, and trafficked to Egypt. The confusion that is undeniably there in the story about exactly how all of this happened, and upon which the writers of *Rev* are playing, is, ironically, typical of a trauma narrative. Traumatized people often have serious difficulties telling the story of what has happened to them, and one of the added indignities of trauma is that often the victims of trauma are not believed because of the gaps and inconsistencies in their stories. I'm not meaning to suggest that the author knew this and deliberately made the story confused. Most scholars think that the confusion is probably the legacy of a couple of different versions of the story being told together here. All I'm noticing is the irony that the recounting of this trauma story happens to display markers that we now understand to be typical of the stories of traumatized people.

Trauma and resilience ...

So that is how Joseph's story begins. One way of reading the rest of Joseph's story is to understand everything that happens next as a consequence of Joseph having been sold into slavery by – well, by whomever it was. Of course, the trafficking of Joseph was caused by the antagonism between him and his brothers, which in turn was caused by Joseph's arrogance and Jacob's unwise favouritism, but it is possible to think about everything that happens to Joseph from this point – and everything that he does – at least partly as being a consequence of his having been trafficked. At each point in the story, we will be asking why Joseph acts in a certain way, or why he doesn't do something you might have expected him to do, and what part his traumatic experiences might be thought to have played.

I'm afraid that at this point I ought to make a confession. I have a job. Yes, all of those applications eventually bore fruit, and I got *a* job. Not *the* job, you'll understand. One of the problems with this job is that it is short-term. It is so short-term, in fact, that it hasn't really stopped the round of applications and interviews; no sooner did it begin than I needed to start thinking about applying for the next job. But this short-term job that I found has turned out to be the reason for this book, and the theme of this short-term job might just turn out to be, I suspect, the dominant theme of the first five years of my big adventure in the UK. That theme is 'trauma'. I have a job as a researcher on a project that is designed to resource clergy to help guide their congregations through the after-effects of trauma. My interest in resilience has come about as a result of my work on this project.

It was uncanny that the project got underway just as a series of major traumas hit London and the UK. Within weeks, and over only a period of a few months, we experienced an attack on Westminster Bridge, another on London Bridge, bombings in Manchester and a London tube station, an attack on a mosque and, perhaps most dramatic and horrifying of all, the Grenfell Tower fire. As a research team, we have spoken first-hand with people who experienced these disasters and with clergy whose unenviable responsibility it has been to minister to their people through them.

Our interest in resilience has come about as a result of this work, as one of the outcomes of an experience of trauma can be increased levels of resilience. Trauma, as I've already said, affects people in different ways. It can be absolutely devastating, and in Chapter 2, as I tell the story of Joseph's early experiences of slavery in Egypt, I'll say some more about the painful, and sometimes bizarre, effects of trauma. But trauma, if one has the opportunity to respond to it well, can also have some positive effects. Going through the process of trauma and coming out the other end can be a little like experiencing the refiner's fire – the final product may in some respects be stronger and more beautiful than the original. There is a wonderful practice as part of Japanese work with porcelain called Kintsugi. Kintsugi involves treating broken pottery with a special lacquer dusted with powdered gold. The repaired product features seams of gold that shine in the light and that function to make the pottery stronger. It is also nearly always more interesting than the original. Trauma can be a little like that, if you imagine the gold-work as seams of resilience running through broken, but re-assembled and repaired people. Perhaps you have experienced this for yourself? What would you identify as the golden seams running through your damaged life? Are you aware of them – perhaps even proud of them? Are you aware of them giving you strength, or making you more interesting? In *Abraham: A journey* I described my experience of living with ME/Chronic Fatigue Syndrome (and feeling too exhausted for either work or fun) for getting on toward 20 years. It was a dreadful experience that I wouldn't wish on anybody and that, at times, felt entirely meaningless. Yet overall I can't entirely wish it had never happened, because of the gifts (or seams) of patience, empathy and reflection it brought with it.

So, resilience can be something that comes unbidden as the result of suffering. Most research on resilience is at pains to say that it can also come as the result of concerted, conscious efforts to cultivate it. While there are nearly as many definitions of resilience as there are practitioners in the field, most describe resilience as a 'process' that can be learned and honed, rather than as a 'trait' that one either possesses or lacks. One helpful guide to resilience and resilience-building that takes this approach is the American Psychological Association's publication 'The Road to Resilience' (you'll find the details in the list of further reading at the end this book.) The APA says: 'Resilience is the process of adapting well in the face of adversity, trauma, tragedy, threats or significant sources of stress … It means "bouncing back" from difficult experiences.'

Like many other commentators on resilience, the APA identifies a series of 'factors' that people can cultivate in order to build their levels of resilience. The APA's factors range from building and maintaining good relationships with family and friends to exercising, paying attention to one's feelings and generally taking good care of oneself. Some of the factors regularly suggested for the building of resilience seem, like these, to be matters of general common sense. Others, such as aptitude for flexible retelling of one's life story, for example, may not be things that would suggest themselves to people in the ordinary run of things. Over the course of this book, we will visit and explore a wide range of these factors and how they might, or might not, help to build levels of resilience.

Your resilience journey

I wonder where you are coming from in your journey to resilience. You may be living in the aftermath of a terrible event involving tragedy, bereavement, injury, injustice or betrayal. If so, the fact that you have picked up this book *may* (but see below) mean that you are ready, or on your way to being ready, to take deliberate steps in your thinking and in your actions, to move toward healing and either to return to your life or to begin the hard work of building a new life. You might be ready to start (consciously – the process may already have begun) to sew seams of gold into your broken self.

Alternatively, you may be in the middle of a long or protracted ordeal that demands from you patience and fortitude just to keep going. For some of you, that description could be applied to your work situation. You may require resilience just to keep on getting out of bed and going to work every day, because your work environment is tense or abusive, or because it is, by its very nature, dangerous. On the other hand, your work may simply be boring and repetitive or may not make good use of your skills. Perhaps, like me, you are having trouble finding appropriate work to do and perhaps the financial consequences of that are a cause of stress. You might be living with chronic illness, or caring for somebody who is ill, or visiting someone who is in prison (or serving a prison term yourself). Living with long-term illness requires huge amounts of fortitude, especially if you hope to keep your closest relationships intact! Perhaps your ordeal is loneliness, or some other form of longing or grief, that saps your energy and seems to drain your life of all colour.

On the other hand, you might come to the topic of resilience from another vantage point altogether. If one of the two previous categories applies to you – if you have experienced an acute event, or you are living with chronic stressors – your need for resilience skills and aptitudes will be pressing. But if you are fortunate enough to be simply getting on with life as normal, you may still feel that your life could be greatly improved if you had the skills to navigate and respond to ordinary stresses and strains and to 'bounce back' quickly and cheerfully.

Wherever you currently fit on this spectrum of experience, you stand to benefit by thinking about how you can build your resilience and by putting the theory into practice. Ironically, you may find that doing resilience work comes more easily if you fit into one of the first two categories – if you are recovering from a major event, or living through a protracted period of challenges. That is because you will have more to gain in the moment *and* because experience of disasters and hardships tend *of their nature* to promote resilience. That old aphorism 'whatever doesn't kill you makes you stronger' is pretty much on the money. But don't let that put you off if you're currently getting along pretty well; we can all do with learning about, and practising, resilience in our fast-paced, demanding world.

There is one word of caution, however, that I'd like to speak for those who *are* currently living in the wake of trauma. Listen carefully to what your body is telling you about your readiness to embark on *conscious* resilience-building. It is important that you don't try to short-change yourself by moving on to a new challenge too quickly. One of the things that we sometimes neglect in our Western culture is to give ourselves time for proper lamentation and grieving over disasters and tragedies. Both body and mind need time to process major shocks. Some writers in the field of trauma use Psalm 23's imagery of 'walking through the valley of the shadow of death' about the period following a traumatic event. They emphasize the fact that this 'walk through the deepest and darkest valley' may take a long time – even years. Only traumatized individuals or communities can know how long their walk through the valley needs to be, and only they will know when it is nearing completion. These writers also stress that there is no alternative to doing this walk in its entirety. One cannot go over, under or around the after-effects of trauma, but only through. You can't speed up the recovery process, and attempts to bring it to an end prematurely will likely mean that the unresolved trauma hangs around, becoming a new 'friend', that will find a wide – and sometimes very odd – range of ways of making its presence felt.

You shouldn't take that to mean, if you are currently walking through the valley, that you should stop reading. There is a great deal to learn about the experience of trauma and recovery in Joseph's story. You can very usefully learn more about the trauma-response process that you are currently experiencing and also take a peek at the new directions in which you might choose to walk, when eventually it is time for you to leave the valley – when you might also choose to take Joseph with you as companion and support.

Then Jacob tore his garments …

If we in the West today tend to be allergic to displays of grief and mourning, and resistant to tending sufficiently to our trauma wounds, that is not a criticism that could be made of the ancient Israelites! Chapter 37 of Genesis ends with a particularly graphic display of grief and mourning. When Joseph's 11 brothers present their father with Joseph's distinctive robe, which they have soiled with goat's blood, Jacob immediately recognizes it as Joseph's and his mind fills in all the missing details of Joseph's fate. 'A wild animal has devoured him: Joseph is without doubt torn to pieces,' Jacob cries. (Gen. 37.33) Then follows an extended description of Jacob's lamenting for his son.

> Then Jacob tore his garments, and put sackcloth on his loins, and mourned for his son many days. All his sons and all his daughters sought to comfort him; but he refused to be comforted, and said, 'No, I shall go down to Sheol to my son, mourning.' Thus his father bewailed him. (Gen. 37.34–35)

Note that Jacob's lamenting comprises both words and actions. He tears his garments and dons mourning garb, and he mourns. During the period of mourning, he refuses to be comforted by his children, but maintains that his mourning will end only with the end of his life. Of course, Jacob does eventually end his period of mourning for Joseph (even if he doesn't recover fully from his grief), but in the early days, his mourning fills his entire reality. Even compared with other biblical stories, this account of Jacob's mourning is quite extensive.

We are not very good, as Western, twenty-first century Christians, at lamenting. This is true of churches, on the whole, as well as of individuals. Often our congregations avoid or dodge the reality of disaster by continuing to sing praise songs on Sunday mornings, even after highly traumatic community events. Yet, lamenting after disasters is an important part of the recovery process, of walking through the valley of the shadow of death. If you are not quite sure how to go about lamenting, there is a good book I can recommend – the Psalms. There are more 'lament' psalms than any other single kind of psalm (see Psalms 13, 88 and 120 as just a few examples). Every single one is an authorized official complaint to God. Make them to him with as much unguarded emotion and undignified display as you can muster! Make them in private, and if you are brave, make them in church where your pain can be witnessed, acknowledged and shared by the congregation at the same time as it is heard and seen by God.

If you look closely at the psalms of lament, you will see that most of them end with statements of faith, praise or hope. (Psalm 88 is a glorious exception – grim to the very end.) Scholars have argued about why this is so, but their best explanation seems to be that the very act of lamenting is effective in moving the emotions of the lamenter, so that by the end of a psalm, the person praying it is able, once more, to express faith, praise or hope in God. Once again, it will be up to you, when you are using the psalms in your lamenting, to determine whether you are yet ready, or able, to pray these final verses. Don't go there before you are ready, but stay in the valley of the shadow of death until you sense that it is time to emerge.

What's in a name?

And meanwhile, what of Joseph himself, who is not dead but sold into slavery in Egypt? I am not going to pretend that Joseph was enlightened to the extent that he knew that he needed to spend time recovering 'in the valley' after his betrayal at the hands of his brothers. Nevertheless, the story, ironically, seems to build that downtime in for him. The next chapter of Genesis, Genesis 38, doesn't mention Joseph *at all*. Instead, it focuses on Joseph's brother Judah, the third-eldest of the brothers. Joseph re-enters the story in Genesis 39, but Genesis 38 is all about Judah – the 'brotherly' brother who reasoned that if they were going to dispose of Joseph, they might at least make a profit out of it! (Gen. 37.26–27)

In the next chapter of *this* book, we will read the two next chapters of Genesis. It might seem a little early to be getting to the sex scenes (!), but Chapters 38 and 39 contain two stories of seductions: of Judah in Genesis 38 and of Joseph in Genesis 39. As you might guess, the two seduction stories are related – even though each is about a different brother. You could easily read the two stories and not notice the parallels, but I will help you to draw them out.

There is something else that you might not notice, and that I may need to draw out of the story for you. It has to do with names. We're dealing with three 'J' names here: Jacob, Judah and Joseph. That can be a bit confusing, but there is something rather important about two of these names. You might remember that Jacob is sometimes known by another name: 'Israel'. Jacob was given the name Israel by the mysterious creature with whom he wrestled through the night at Peniel (Gen. 32.28). The name Israel has two other associations in the Old Testament. Sometimes Israel is used to refer to the whole of God's chosen nation, and sometimes it is used to refer to just the northern kingdom, which was centred on Samaria, as distinct from the southern kingdom, Judah, which was centred on Jerusalem. 'Judah', of course, is also another of our three 'J' names. The fact that our story uses two of these significant geographic names is a hint that there is something more to it than just a small, family-oriented drama. This is not just a story about brothers – it is also a story about nations (nations who have split from one another and who experience 'sibling rivalry' just as brothers do), in which each of the characters represents a large body of people. The story operates on both levels at once. At one level it asks, 'which brother will succeed Jacob and become the patriarch to lead the family into the next generation?' If you have read *Abraham: A journey*, you will know that all of Genesis is built on this recurring theme: 'which son shall be chosen?' At the other level, the level of nations, the story asks 'which nation will come out on top – Judah (south) or Israel (north)?' In the story, Judah represents the south (Judah), and Joseph represents the north (Israel). In the next chapter of *this* book, we will begin to see the political story that is developing as Judah and Joseph battle it out to be both chosen son *and* chosen nation.

Perhaps this political element of the story hasn't come as a surprise to you. After all, *each one* of Jacob's sons becomes one of the 12 tribes of Israel, and each tribe is eventually given its own allotted portion of land, with the half-tribes of Ephraim and Manasseh (the sons of Joseph) receiving allotments of land in the north, and the other tribes in the south. So it is entirely possible that you already associate Joseph with the north in your mind. But it may equally be possible that you have previously overlooked the political and geographical elements of the Joseph saga, as the 12 sons – but primarily Joseph and Judah – struggle for pre-eminence.

Before we leave this discussion about names, I should say that there is one name that has not come up at all so far in this first chapter. And that name is 'God'. God is by no means entirely absent from Joseph's story, but *is* absent from Genesis 37 (unless you consider God to have been responsible for Joseph's dreams, to which we will turn in a moment). Unusually, not even one of the characters speaks God's name in Genesis 37. I should confess that God does not play a terrifically obvious role in the whole Joseph saga, and this is a theme that we shall be returning to, and pondering, over the course of the book.

However, that is not the case for Chapters 38 and 39 of Genesis, our focus in the next chapter. Especially in Genesis 39, it is as if God storms out of nowhere to become, suddenly, the name on every-body's lips. And that is something that we shall need to ponder also. But just for now, I want to whet your appetite for a little bit of mystery (as well as the sex scenes!) by telling you that God is referred to by a different name in Genesis 38 and 39 than in the rest of the Joseph saga. Elsewhere, the Hebrew word used to refer to God is 'Elohim', a native Canaanite word meaning 'gods' (yes, it's plural), but used in the Old Testament as a proper name for God (that mostly takes singular verbs). 'Elohim' is translated in most English translations simply as 'God'. In Genesis 38 and 39, however, God is referred to almost exclusively as 'YHWH'. This unpronounceable collection of consonants (scholars pronounce it as 'Yahweh'), based on the Hebrew verb 'to be', is the special divine name that is first made known to the Israelites in Exodus 3. 'YHWH' is translated in most English translations as 'the LORD' and when read aloud in Hebrew, is often pronounced 'Adonai' (meaning 'Lord') in order to avoid speaking the divine name. There is just one exception to the use of this special name in Genesis 38 and 39 – in Genesis 39.9, Joseph speaks of God using the name 'Elohim'. If you look up Genesis 38 and 39 in your Bible, however, you will see the name 'the LORD' everywhere (especially in Genesis 39) and the name 'God' in this one place only.

What does this use of the special divine name YHWH in Genesis 38 and 39 signify? And how, if at all, does it relate to the three 'J' names and the two levels of the story – family saga and national history – that are connected to those names? That will be for us to wrestle with in Chapter Two.

The Dreamer

To draw an end to this first chapter, I want to return to its title. The dreamer of the title is, of course, Joseph. His story begins with his two dreams of greatness. In the first, Joseph and his brothers are binding sheaves in a field when the brothers' sheaves of wheat bow down to Joseph's sheaf. In the second dream, the sun, the moon and 11 stars (corresponding to Joseph's 11 brothers) bow down before Joseph. Joseph tells the first dream only to his brothers, but he tells the second to his father, Jacob, also. The dreams, predictably, make Joseph's brothers hate him and stir up their jealousy, but Jacob stores the dream away for future reference – and you might like to do the same.

Already, though, you might be thinking about Joseph's dreams a little differently from the way you thought about them at the beginning of this chapter – seeing them now as more than just the puffed-up (or even divinely inspired) aspirations of the second youngest son of a large family. The political battle for supremacy between the tribes is also being signalled here. The first dream even uses the language of kings and kingdoms: 'reigning' and 'having dominion' over people. Right from the beginning, this is a story of political intrigue and machinations.

This dual nature of the story – family story and national history – is going to help us to think about trauma, and resilience as response to it, in a very broad way in this book. We will be thinking both about the resilience of individuals and the resilience of whole nations – in some chapters one more than the other, and in other chapters, both.

But just for now I want you to think briefly about resilience and dreams. Do the two go together? Is having a dream necessary for building resilience? We will need to read on to start to develop answers to those questions, but another lot of questions you are equipped to answer right now. Do you have a dream? What is it? Have you shared it? Is it a dream that family and friends can get behind, or is it more likely to stir up envy or hatred? Probably you have a number of dreams that operate at a number of different levels, as in Joseph's story. To what extent do they help you to keep on putting one foot in front of the other – to 'bounce back' from adversity?

The dream with which I am beginning this book is my dream of finding a full-time, permanent job in my newly adopted homeland. Previously, my dream had been to find a husband. With that dream now realized (see *Abraham: A journey* for the full story!), my dream has changed. Of course, there are other dreams also – that R. and I will make a home near my new work, that we and our families will be healthy and challenged and fulfilled, and that we will live out our days in the service and love of God. Oh, and knocking away in the back of my mind somewhere is a long-neglected dream of turning into a sultry jazz diva. As I'm writing, these are all still dreams. Will they be fulfilled? I will need to keep writing and you to keep reading.

2
The seduction

GENESIS 38—39

Now Joseph was taken down to Egypt, and Potiphar, an officer
of Pharaoh, the captain of the guard, an Egyptian, bought
him from the Ishmaelites who had brought him down there.
[2] The LORD was with Joseph, and he became a successful man.
(Gen. 39.1–2)

However resilience is defined, its central feature seems to be a capacity to 'bounce back' after setbacks. Resilience allows a person to take
stresses and strains in their stride and to continue on. This doesn't
necessarily mean that he or she doesn't feel the cost or pain of a difficult or traumatic experience, or take some time out to come to terms
with it, but just that the resilient person is able to pull themselves up
afterwards and to continue on – perhaps noticing that the difficult
experience has made them stronger, in some respect, than they had
been before.

As you are embarking on this journey, how would you assess your
own levels of resilience? Do you feel like a new-ish rubber band that
easily springs back into shape after it has been pulled tight? Or do you
feel that some (or all) of your elasticity has gone (perhaps like that in
your more ancient underwear), so that each time you are stretched,
you find it harder and harder to get back to something near your
original shape? I quite often hear older people say that they no longer
feel as resilient as they used to, but that age and experience has worn
them down so that bouncing back seems to require more and more
energy. But age is not the only thing that might cause you to feel less

resilient than you'd like to be. If you are currently dealing with a major setback – if you (or a family member) have just been given a worrying medical prognosis, for example – you might find that you have difficulty brushing off things that might have seemed relatively minor prior to the diagnosis. The same would be true, of course, if you are currently mourning a death, or a missed job opportunity, or the end of a relationship or any one of a number of other major misfortunes. Alternatively, it might not be just one major event that is whittling away your resilience levels. If you have a job, or a family life, that requires constantly high levels of patience or exposes you to constant stress or violence, you may find over time that your resilience levels decrease and need some conscious attention. Ironically, I often find that if I have been living in a situation like that, I can cope so long as things are bad or demanding. Once the situation and the stressors have eased, however, I sometimes feel that I have no resilience left. I collapse in a heap and feel annoyed with myself and confused about why I should suddenly fall apart *now*.

In the last chapter, we met Joseph and read the story of his very major setback. By the end of Chapter 37 of Genesis, Joseph has been betrayed by his brothers, bought and sold by groups of passing strangers, and finally trafficked to Egypt and sold to Potiphar, one of Pharaoh's officers and the captain of his guard. How does Joseph cope with all of this? As I mentioned at the end of Chapter One, at this point Joseph gets 'left on ice' by the editors of Genesis for a whole chapter, while they tell the story of the seduction of Joseph's elder brother Judah. I suggested that this narrative manoeuvre unwittingly respects Joseph's need for time to lament and 'walk through the valley of the shadow'. It also, of course, leaves readers like you and me hanging in suspense, waiting to find out what is going to happen to Joseph! Unlike the editors of Genesis, we're going to carry on with Joseph's story straight away and come back to Judah later. His story will actually make more sense to us once we know what happens to Joseph.

We might have expected to find Joseph in a bad situation or in low spirits. Surprisingly, however, when we reconnect with Joseph, we see that he appears to have fallen on his feet (or 'bounced back'). You will recall that Joseph had been very successful at winning the special favour of his father, Jacob. Now he proves to be just as successful at winning the special favour of his new Egyptian master, Potiphar. Potiphar puts Joseph in charge of his household. The Hebrew text of Genesis 39.4 says that Potiphar *gave everything he had into Joseph's hand*. Potiphar seems to have been so confident in the skills of his new slave that he felt able to pass all his domestic responsibilities on to Joseph, so that after Joseph's arrival, Potiphar 'had no concern for anything but the food that he ate'. (Gen. 39.6)

I also said toward the end of Chapter One that God makes a sudden appearance in the story at this point. In Genesis 39, God and God's influence are very much in evidence, as we shall see. God proves to be very present in Joseph's life, causing Joseph to prosper ('YHWH was with Joseph and he became a successful man' Gen 39.2) and blessing all of Potiphar's undertakings for Joseph's sake ('YHWH blessed the Egyptian's house for Joseph's sake; the blessing of YHWH was on all that he had, in house and field' Gen 39.5). Surprisingly, the Egyptian Potiphar knows Joseph's God and even knows, and uses, God's special name, YHWH. Potiphar recognizes YHWH's presence with Joseph. We will see, as we work our way through Genesis 39, that God stays close to Joseph throughout the chapter – even when, as is about to be the case, everything goes suddenly rather badly.

Do you have any particular reaction to God's becoming part of the story at this point? Is it reassuring? A relief? Or curious? Or annoying? And how do you feel about Joseph's return to prosperity? Are you relieved for him, or are you wondering why God has picked him out for special favour? And do your feelings raise any theological questions for you? Throughout the chapter, God's presence with Joseph continues to be linked closely with Joseph's prosperity and with the power and authority he's given. How you respond to that may depend a little on how you think about what is sometimes termed the 'prosperity gospel' – the idea that relationship with God leads to worldly prosperity. Keep an eye on your reactions as we progress through the story.

At the beginning of this part of the story, then, we find Joseph, perhaps surprisingly, appearing to be in rather good shape. That makes it all the more surprising when everything very suddenly unravels. On the surface, Joseph appears to be powerful, but events transpire that make it apparent that his situation is in fact rather vulnerable, and Joseph finds himself on the horns of a very modern dilemma.

Potiphar's wife begins to pursue Joseph. We read in Genesis 39.6 that Joseph was 'handsome and good-looking'. In the very next verse, Genesis 39.7, Potiphar's wife casts her eye on Joseph, and she says to him, 'Lie with me'. Potiphar might have given Joseph almost all of his own power and wealth, but with Mrs Potiphar's curt demand, all of Joseph's newly found prosperity is threatened and his power exposed as illusory. He's damned if he does and damned if he doesn't. If he lies with Potiphar's wife and Potiphar finds out, he could be removed from his position of authority and punished severely. If he doesn't lie with Potiphar's wife, she could find ways to make his life just as difficult – they appear to occupy the house together, in Potiphar's absence, quite regularly. Joseph's power is real, but it is vulnerable in this one area, where his master and his master's wife may not see eye to eye. What will he do?

#MeToo

We are living in the aftermath of the Weinstein saga and the #MeToo movement, and I have found it fascinating to be thinking about Joseph's story in that context. Joseph's may be an ancient story, but its themes are pretty up to date! Just as Genesis 39 deals with issues of power and how sexuality can be *used* to exploit power and can be *experienced* as undermining power, so too the cases of sexual abuse within the film industry, politics and other high-profile spheres that have become public in recent months have revolved around issues of power. Women actors, for example, have spoken about the kinds of sexual abuse that they have sometimes felt pressured to undergo for the sake of establishing or protecting their careers. Arguably, sexual abuse is always about power and about inequality of power, at one level or another.

Why do I think that Mrs Potiphar's attempted seduction of Joseph is about power? It does, after all, come immediately after the reader is told of Joseph's beauty for the first time. Couldn't it be that Mrs Potiphar is motivated simply by attraction, or by lust? The clue that this seduction attempt is about power comes in Mrs Potiphar's demand: 'lie with me!' This speech is very bald – it has none of the marks of the politeness that usually embellish sexual propositions in the Old Testament. Even Judah's proposition to a woman he presumes to be a prostitute in Genesis 38 (which we'll come back to shortly) contains the word 'please' in the Hebrew. The bald phrase 'lie with me' appears only one other time in the Old Testament – in the story of Amnon's rape of his sister Tamar. We're going to come back to that one later too.

One of the interesting elements of Joseph's story, of course, is that it is about attempted sexual abuse of a *man* by a *woman*. While it is certainly not the case today that all sexual abuse is practised upon women by men, the focus in the current round of debates has been on women's experience of sexual abuse. The #MeToo campaign has encouraged women to acknowledge and name their experiences of abuse, on the grounds that to do so exposes the prevalence of abuse and also goes some way to reducing the stigma experienced by survivors. Like many women, I have had mixed feelings about the campaign. Partly, I mistrust anything that encourages people to jump on the particular bandwagon of the moment, especially if it means targeting another group, like men in this case. Nevertheless, I also see the importance of acknowledging the extent of the problem and bringing facts to light that will discourage tolerance of the casual abuse of power against women.

The campaign has also brought something home to me that has surprised me. Initially, I thought that I didn't have a particular story to share as part of the campaign. I could think of one or two instances of sexually inappropriate behaviour being directed at me, but I felt that I had got off lightly and that my stories were relatively insignificant when compared with those of other women. When I thought at greater length, however, I remembered several experiences about which I could justifiably have complained. I remembered the 'uncle' who repeatedly put his hand on my upper back, inside my t-shirt, while ostensibly pointing out southern hemisphere constellations with his other hand, and that I had felt uncomfortable about this, but unable to tell anybody. I remembered the head of department who had spoken to me highly inappropriately (and inaccurately, as it happens) about my sexuality during my first weeks in a new job and the choice that I faced between reporting him (with likely serious consequences for him and for my workplace) or simply managing the relationship going forward. (I chose the latter.) And I remembered the handful of male colleagues and friends who had contrived to made it clear to me, one way or another, that although they had no intention of leaving their partners or wives, they wanted to get as close to me as possible under the circumstances and were prepared to play a little dirty in order to bring that about. More than one of these latter experiences proved to have long-term consequences for my health and well-being, and each was excruciating in its own way.

You might well agree with my first assessment – I've got off lightly! Yet each situation was painful, and each saw me at some point curled up on my bed in the foetal position, feeling responsible and guilty. In each of these situations, I experienced vulnerability. In the first, I was a child, staying in the home of a family friend. In the second, I was in my first days in a workplace, which would be forever changed were I to complain. The third, I suspect, is one of the in-built hazards of being a long-term singleton.

It is also true that in each of these situations, I had some degree of power and agency. The first example was tricky for a pre-teen, but I could have got word to my mother. In the second, I realized that I possessed power in frankly frightening amounts and that how I chose to wield it would likely have significant ramifications for many people and for an institution. (Looking back, subsequent events suggest that my decision not to report has indeed had significant ramifications for at least half a dozen other people, whose lives would in all likelihood be different today had I exercised my power more publicly and blown the whistle.) The third example is the most complex, and the most compromising, and of course each story was different. I may have been single, and I may have been experiencing manipulation, but I could (and did, eventually) act to take myself out of each of these situations, having suffered (and no doubt caused or been complicit in) varying degrees of harm to myself and others.

No woman should have to suffer the various abuses I've described, and yet the sobering truth is that most have experienced far worse. Action is required to right the wrongs of the past. But the danger for #MeToo is that it risks encouraging women to embrace their vulnerabilities and to self-identify as victims. At first blush, that might not sound to you to be such a bad thing. However, I am hoping you might want to rethink that assessment, if it is yours, at the end of the chapter. I am hoping to demonstrate that as much as lamenting and walking through the valley of the shadow are vital to building resilience and to recovering from injuries, adopting the attitude of a victim is not.

I had begun to note above that one of the interesting things about Mrs Potiphar's seduction of Joseph is that it is an exercise of sexual power by a woman against a man. That scenario too is an issue today – as is abuse by and against trans and non-gender-binary people. The 'gender-switch' element of Joseph's story, however, leads to a particularly heightened degree of vulnerability for him because of the context of the times in which his story is told. To find out why, we need to continue on with the story.

What Joseph does next …

At first Joseph successfully resists Mrs Potiphar's repeated advances. In fact, he does extraordinarily well initially. He stands up to her and responds directly:

> Look, with me here, my master has no concern about anything in the house, and he has put everything that he has in my hand. He is not greater in this house than I am, nor has he kept back anything from me except yourself, because you are his wife. How then could I do this great wickedness, and sin against God? (Gen. 39.8–9)

Joseph responds honourably, and it is partly his conduct here that has led to his reputation for righteousness. We are not told in the story how Joseph felt about Mrs Potiphar or how he felt about her advances – only that he turned them down in a respectful and pious way. Perhaps he didn't find her attractive? It is impossible to know for certain whether his responses reflect righteousness or just simply lack of interest! As is often the case in Genesis stories, the text doesn't give away the details of how the characters are feeling.

But Mrs Potiphar is determined. She waits until a day when Joseph is working in the house and they are alone. She catches hold of his garment, again saying 'lie with me!' This time, Joseph can't talk his way out of it. He flees from her, leaving his garment in her hand. Mrs Potiphar goes into damage control. Seeing that Joseph has fled, leaving his garment, she calls out to her other house servants and tells them that *Joseph* had tried to seduce *her*, but that he had fled after she had lifted up her voice and cried out. The servants apparently believe her, and she plans the next part of her subterfuge. Keeping Joseph's garment by her side, she waits for Potiphar to return home at the end of the day. When Potiphar arrives, she tells him the same story she told the servants, brandishing the garment as evidence. Again, Mrs Potiphar is successful. Potiphar believes her story, he becomes enraged and he throws Joseph into prison.

Joseph's humiliation is complete. He is stripped of the honour and authority he had initially won from Potiphar and becomes not only a slave but a prisoner too. Two details, however, suggest that this may not mark the absolute end of Joseph's rise to power. First, this is not an ordinary jail, but the jail where the prisoners of the king are kept. Secondly, various themes from the beginning of the chapter recur. Once again, we hear that YHWH is with Joseph and causes him to prosper (Gen. 39.21, 23). Joseph finds favour in the eyes of the chief jailer (just as he had done with Jacob and Potiphar), who puts all the prisoners under Joseph's care and all things under his authority (Gen. 39.21–22). The chapter ends, then, as it began, with Joseph apparently in desperate straits (first as slave and then a prisoner), but winning the confidence of his master and being given almost unfettered authority in his new context.

If Joseph's situation is almost the same after Mrs Potifar's attempted seduction as it had been before it, why is the seduction a part of the story and what is being telegraphed to the reader by means of its inclusion? You could argue that nothing really happens in Chapter 39! Joseph begins as a *slave* with authority and privilege and ends as a *prisoner* with authority and privilege. However, the reader learns along the way that Joseph can be a charming character – he has shown himself capable of charming just about any superior and earning their trust. The reader also learns that God's presence remains constant through this experience. Joseph doesn't win power and influence people all on his own – YHWH plays an important role. And of course, the story does progress. At the beginning, Joseph charms and wins over the head of a domestic household. By the end, he has charmed and won over the head of one of Pharaoh's institutions. He is inching his way toward Pharaoh.

He's such a girl …

What does all of this imply about Joseph's resilience? Is Mrs. Potiphar's attempted seduction something that Joseph just sails through? Is that what resilience means, that the resilient person walks through potentially difficult experiences without suffering any appreciable distress? And what about the impact of his experience of being trafficked? Should we just expect Joseph to have recovered and to be ready to move on to the next thing? I want to share with you a few clues in the text that suggest that the impact of Mrs Potiphar's sexual abuse of Joseph exposes his vulnerabilities more than you might immediately imagine.

You may recall I said that one other Old Testament character uses the 'bald' entreaty 'Lie with me!' It is David's son Amnon, shortly before he rapes his half-sister Tamar in 2 Samuel 13. Amnon falls in love with Tamar, but he doesn't know how to win her. His 'crafty' friend Jonadab suggests that Amnon should pretend to be ill and ask Tamar to bring some food to his chamber and feed him by hand. They would then be alone and in close physical proximity. Amnon does this, and the plan works – more or less. When Amnon says 'Lie with me!' Tamar responds in a manner not unlike Joseph. She confronts the situation directly, refusing Amnon and begging him not to force her. She warns her brother about the consequences should he take her by force, and she begs him instead to approach the king to request his consent for their marriage (2 Sam. 13:13). But Amnon refuses to listen to her and rapes her. Afterwards, we learn, Amnon is seized with a hatred for his half-sister even stronger than his previous love. 'Get out!' he tells her, with his customary grace. Tamar objects that this dishonour is worse than the first, but Amnon has his servants put her outside and bolt the door against her. At this point the text adds a slightly odd note – some translations put it in brackets, thus: '(Now she was wearing a long robe with sleeves: for this is how the virgin daughters of the king were clothed in earlier times)' (2 Sam. 13:18). The narrator tells us that Tamar rips this robe, puts ashes on her head and goes away crying aloud. Her other brother, Absalom, offers her the helpful advice that, because Amnon is her brother, she should 'be quiet for now' and not take the matter to heart. However, you should note that after their father, King David, refuses to punish Amnon, his much-loved firstborn child, Absalom takes the matter very much to heart indeed. Meanwhile, Tamar remains 'a desolate woman in her brother Absalom's house' (2 Sam. 13.20).

Have you noticed some parallels between the stories of Tamar and Joseph? Both characters have a certain amount of power and authority (Joseph in the house of his master and Tamar as the daughter of the king), which is undermined by the unwanted approaches of another. Both are sexually ambushed in the chamber of a person whom they are serving. And both have fathers who play favourites among their children with disastrous results. But there is one further parallel that you may not have noticed, because it is only really there in the Hebrew. The description of Tamar's robe in 2 Sam. 13.18 is identical to that of Joseph's robe in Genesis 37. Andrew Lloyd-Webber's musical means that we will always think of Joseph's robe as a 'technicolor dreamcoat', but in fact the Hebrew means something more like 'a coat with sleeves'. Tamar is the only other Old Testament character to wear one, although the odd comment in brackets in her story tells us that it was traditionally the garment worn by 'the virgin daughters of the king'. Without this detail, you could notice the parallels between the two stories as a curiosity, but this parallel, together with the common entreaty 'Lie with me!', must very probably mean that the authors of the two stories wished to connect them and to bring both into the minds of their readers. One effect, for readers of the Joseph story, is to thoroughly feminize Joseph. First, his father clothes him in the garb of a princess, and subsequently he is pursued and seduced as though he were a virgin girl.

I want to come back to Joseph's symbolic feminization and its significance in a moment, but let me highlight one other interesting feature of Joseph's story. I've said that Potiphar was an 'officer' and the captain of the guard. The Hebrew word that most English Bible translations translate as 'officer' also means 'eunuch' – indeed it is arguable that 'eunuch' is its primary meaning (and many of the servants of Pharaoh and other ancient leaders *were* eunuchs). Some interpreters of the story have read Joseph's story with this alternative translation in mind. They suggest that it may be the case that Potiphar and his wife, far from being at odds over Joseph, were in collusion, and that one of Potiphar's goals in purchasing Joseph was that he should sire a son for them! On this interpretation, Mrs Potiphar was merely acting according to the plan, until the plan was ruined by Joseph's refusal to cooperate. These scholars argue that after Joseph's refusal, Mrs Potiphar had to make a public show about Joseph's disrespect in order to save face in front of the servants. Now, inevitably there is more to the argument, which you may or may not find convincing on the basis of the little I've shared with you here. But what is fascinating about this reading is that it builds a surprising parallel with another Genesis story. In Genesis 16, Abraham and Sarah are finding it difficult to conceive a child together. Sarah solves the problem by suggesting that Abraham lie with her Egyptian slave-woman, Hagar. Hagar duly conceives and gives birth to Ishmael. We know that it doesn't go well after that! But think about Joseph's situation – we might have here a childless *Egyptian* couple who want to co-opt their *Hebrew* slave to have their child – and once again Joseph is cast in the role of the woman. (I'll bet you never thought about Sarah and Mrs Potiphar together in that light before!)

In ancient Israelite culture (and in the cultures of the surrounding nations), gender was significant and rigid. Almost the greatest insult to a man was that he should be likened to a woman. Victors in armed combat would often 'emasculate' their defeated enemies in order to shame them, by shaving their beards and cutting off their garments at the hips, as in 2 Sam. 10.4–5, for example. It is likely that the antipathy to sex between men in some parts of the Old Testament is attributable to this conception of the shame of the man who appears feminine or who functions sexually in the role of a woman. Men were people of power and authority who 'possessed' women as daughters, wives, etc. To give up that authority by taking on the role of a woman was seen as a matter of great shame. It is against this background that we need to consider the fate of Joseph in Genesis 39 – he is pursued sexually by a woman whose authority exceeds his own, in circumstances which cast him in the role of 'sexual slave' or 'princess'.

Now, one might argue that the outcomes in Joseph's story and Tamar's are very different, and that perhaps this is the point of the parallel. While Tamar succumbs to the seduction, Joseph flees and avoids physical abuse. Is the parallel designed to emphasize Joseph's virtue in resisting Mrs Potiphar's advances? Perhaps this is the case – although I'd be *extremely* hesitant about suggesting that the parallel was, conversely, designed to impugn Tamar by suggesting that she should have done more to resist her abuser. Nevertheless, my own small experiences, described above, were sufficiently painful to leave me in little doubt that not only Tamar, but Joseph also, would have been seriously scarred by these sexual assaults, whether consummated or not. And there are clues in the story to suggest that Joseph was, in any event, still affected significantly by the trauma of his trafficking experience. In order to show you those clues, I will first need to share with you a little more about the effects of trauma upon the body and the brain, and their impact upon thinking about resilience.

The compulsion to repeat

Trauma is strange. Trauma affects the body and mind in ways that you wouldn't credit if you didn't have direct experience of it. As I've already noted, trauma has a tendency to bypass the thinking brain. When a person experiences something that is too overwhelming for the brain to comprehend, the person never *really* 'experiences' the traumatic event, and the event is not stored in the person's memory but elsewhere in their body. That is why people 'forget', or find it hard to talk about, traumatic events and why those events have a habit of turning up later as flashbacks. Again, as I've said, all of this is the body's own protection mechanism in action, but it can nevertheless lead to very serious problems if not resolved over time.

One of the strangest things that has been observed about trauma is a phenomenon sometimes termed 'the compulsion to repeat'. When a person gets 'stuck' in trauma response over a long period of time, the brain has a tendency to attempt to re-create the traumatic experience, in the 'hope' that the event will eventually be resolved in a way that the brain can handle. An example of this phenomenon is that people who have been traumatized by motor vehicle accidents sometimes find themselves having further accidents, which may even occur on the same stretch of road and/or on the same day of the calendar year as the original accident! Even though this sounds bizarre, you might know somebody to whom that has happened. R., for example, had an accident one year around Halloween, when he was pulled out of the wreckage of his overturned car. He has often experienced anxiety around that time of year – which has even resulted in him having other accidents, such as falling off his motorbike! The phenomenon doesn't only happen with motor vehicle accidents, however. People re-create the most complicated scenarios of all descriptions (completely unwittingly) in order to attempt to resolve all kinds of traumas, and these 're-enactments' have the potential to be devastating to the innocent people who happen to be standing too close and who get caught up in them. It is important to stress that the traumatized person is responding to an entirely unconscious compulsion – they do not know what they are doing and would likely be genuinely amazed if a professional were to point it out to them.

It probably sounds crazy, but the hallmarks of the compulsion to repeat can be found in numerous places in the Joseph saga, including the story of Mrs Potiphar's attempted seduction in Genesis 39. You might be as surprised as I was to discover that there are some strange parallels between this story and the story of Joseph's betrayal by his brothers. Let's go back to that earlier story for a moment. Joseph is exploited by people who want to take advantage of him (his brothers want to get rid of him and hope they might make some money in the process). He winds up trapped (in a pit). He is stripped naked (of the 'robe-with-sleeves'), and his garment is used as false evidence about him (to persuade his father that he's been attacked by a wild animal). In the Mrs Potiphar episode, Joseph is again exploited by someone who wants to take advantage of him (Mrs Potiphar either wants a dalliance or his children). He winds up trapped (in a prison). He is stripped naked (when Joseph flees Mrs Potiphar's bed chamber, he leaves his garment in her hand), and the garment is used as false evidence against him (by Mrs Potiphar, who uses it to persuade the servants and her husband that Joseph tried to seduce her).

Don't get me wrong, I'm not trying to argue that the biblical authors knew about the compulsion to repeat and wrote it into the story! (Although it is possible that they observed the phenomenon on some level and reflected it in their writing.) I'm not even trying to suggest that Joseph somehow engineered the whole encounter with his master's wife. I simply want to draw your attention to this story as an illustration of how unresolved trauma can continue to reverberate in a person's life. Later on, we'll see some further examples of the compulsion to repeat that will seem clearer and, hopefully, make more sense. But the point of this example is that it points to Joseph's vulnerability, even in the midst of his apparent early success in Egypt in winning the approval and trust of the authority figures he encounters – Potiphar and the chief jailer.

Victims and victimizers

The compulsion to repeat is, unfortunately, part of the same brain mechanism that predisposes victims of trauma to victimize others. You will probably be aware that the perpetrators of sexual abuse against children have a tendency to have been abused themselves as children. On a rational level, that makes very little sense. A person who has experienced abuse as a child knows exactly the kind, and severity, of harm that can be caused thereby. The fact is that this is not rational at all. The child who has been abused knows intimately only two life roles: abuser and abused. Some will go on to suffer further abuse. Others, unfortunately, go on to abuse, and it is all tied up with this subconscious compulsion to repeat, which in turn is tied up with a subconscious desire to 'heal' the original trauma. I should stress, of course, that it is quite possible for victims of child sexual abuse to transcend this behavioural pattern, but it generally takes concerted effort through counselling and other forms of treatment for trauma.

The well-documented phenomenon by which the abused person is statistically more likely to go on to abuse others is one of the reasons why the identification of unresolved trauma in the character of Joseph – even, or especially, in the context of his successes – is important. Without wanting to give the game away too much, what we are going to see as we read on into the Joseph story are some very strong suggestions that this abused boy may go on to become an abuser himself.

This same phenomenon is also the reason why I have concerns about #MeToo. Identifying oneself closely with one's vulnerabilities and past injuries or injustices can sometimes help to build one's resilience in the short term, but over time it tends to undermine rather than to build up, and it also has a propensity to lead to new instances of abuse. Sensitivity to injury and injustice, unfortunately, has a tendency to grow and develop when not kept in careful check. The assertion of a right not to be raped can, for example, morph into an assertion of a right not to be touched or looked at inappropriately, which can turn into an assertion of a right not to be *'made' to feel uncomfortable.* As such notions of 'rights' develop and change and are, over time, applied to behaviour that is less and less extreme, paradoxically, the level of 'offence' caused by breaches tends to grow. The nadir is reached when it is felt to be no longer 'safe' to confront offenders, or when conversation is deemed pointless on the grounds that, for example, a man could not possibly understand the context from which a woman is speaking or have anything of value to speak into it.

Contrary to some of the rhetoric of the women's movement, it is not necessarily 'strong' or 'empowered' to refuse conversation and reconciliation with men on the grounds that it is either dangerous or pointless. It may, on the contrary, be excessively sensitive, and it may be abusive. And it is unlikely to be resilient. While it is undoubtedly important to identify and redress injustices when we see them, to be totally caught up in the injustices done to *ourselves*, whether individually or as a group, is damaging both to ourselves and to the people we unintentionally harm.

Well, I may have gone out on a limb there! If I have, it is as a result of my experiences over the last five years in England, where I have watched these dynamics play themselves out in academia and elsewhere, including churches. I'm afraid that the stories connected with these experiences are not mine to tell, and so I will need to ask you to measure my observations against your own experiences and observations. Have I simply got the women's movement wrong and betrayed the sisterhood, or do you hear in what I'm suggesting some reverberations with things you also have observed? What are *your* stories, even if you are like me and perhaps not the person authorized to tell them?

I have one final observation on this point, and it is an important one. I have considered Joseph's story so far entirely from Joseph's perspective and not from Mrs Potiphar's. To be fair, this is a short-coming of the text as well as of my reading of it. I have focused a great deal on how Joseph's previous experiences and trauma may have influenced his actions. But how might Mrs Potiphar's experiences and past traumas have led her, first, to attempt to seduce Joseph and, then, to accuse him of the very same? We don't know a great deal about her, except that she is apparently childless and married to a man who cannot give her children. Her husband is close to power, but essentially a functionary. He is possibly also weak – certainly, she seems to have him wrapped around her little finger. What is it that has driven her to take the easy option – finger-pointing at a slave – rather than facing her own demons?

What, then, have we learned about resilience so far? Much of it so far is, I'm afraid, a lesson in what resilience is *not*. Resilience is not just sailing through a negative experience and carrying on as if nothing has happened. It is not about 'soldiering on'. The resilient person will pause and reflect on the self-care that will be needed in order to 'bounce back' from a negative experience. This process may be lengthy and may involve lamentation and standing up to an injustice. We've seen that failing to take this kind of self-care can be dangerous for individuals, predisposing them to experience further traumas. We've also seen that a failure to take this kind of self-care can be dangerous to others, predisposing them to experience further traumas at the hand of the individual. On the flip side, we've also seen that resilience is not about becoming ever more sensitive to perceived injustices and hedging oneself around with ever more protective walls of rights. Somewhere (!) there is a line between appropriate self-care and over-identification with injury. Vulnerability deserves attention, but not fixation. Finding that line is part of what resilience is all about. In Chapter Three, you may be pleased to hear, we will be looking more closely at what resilience *is* than what it *is not*.

Where is God in this?

The most important thing remaining for us to do in this chapter is to think about the role that God plays in the story. In order to do so effectively, we first need to explore some different ways of reading Scripture, as God's presence with Joseph in Genesis 39 poses something of an interpretational problem. The problem, put simply, is that God is prominent in this chapter, but nowhere else in Joseph's story. We noted God's absence already in Genesis 37 and began to ask some questions about what that absence might reflect. As we go on, we'll find that God's absence is a feature of the rest of Joseph's story too. Here, in Genesis 39, however, God is very present, and Joseph's success is attributed to that presence.

One way of reading Scripture can be described as 'horizontal', or as some scholars call it, 'synchronic'. A synchronic reading is one that focuses on the text as we have it today and tries to make sense of it, even the bits that might appear strange or problematic. In a synchronic reading of the Joseph saga, we are likely to ask questions about why God is active in this part of the story and not in the rest. We might wonder, for example, whether perhaps Joseph does something in the course of this chapter to lose God's presence and special favour. One possible argument against that interpretation would be that the story just doesn't say so! It doesn't identify anything that Joseph does or doesn't do to lose God's favour, and it doesn't say that God withdraws from Joseph. It is just the case that God is part of the action in one part of the story and not in the rest. Another possible argument, and the one I'd favour, is that in this story God is present with Joseph precisely when Joseph needs God's presence the most. The early days after Joseph's trafficking to Egypt, when he first begins his life as a slave, are, I've argued, when he is at his most vulnerable. It is in this time that he needs God the most, and this is the time when God is present with him. If this reading satisfies you, then this is one way you could understand God's role in the story.

Another way of reading Scripture can be described as 'vertical', or as some scholars call it, 'diachronic'. A diachronic reading is one that asks questions about the history of the text that we have today. It makes educated guesses about how the text reached its current form and how it might have been different at different times in the past. For example, clues in the text may suggest that at some earlier time, bits of text were added or changed. Such clues can include repetition of details, inconsistencies, changes in language, style, or perspective, or abrupt shifts from one subject to another. One type of clue like this is 'resumption'. Resumption occurs when a story that ends abruptly at one point resumes later, sometimes with the repeating of important detail. There is an example in Genesis 39. Genesis 37 ends by saying that Joseph was sold in Egypt to Potiphar. It is followed by Chapter 38, which tells an apparently completely unrelated story. Genesis 39 begins by repeating the details of Joseph's sale to Potiphar. What that suggests to scholars is that Chapter 38 may have been added later and that the necessary changes were made to ensure the smooth running of the story from Chapters 37 to 39.

Another clue that Genesis 38 was added later is that it uses God's special name – YHWH. As I've already said, Genesis 39 also uses the distinctive name YHWH, and yet, apart from these two chapters, the name YHWH doesn't appear anywhere else in the Joseph story (apart from one instance in Genesis 49.18, another passage that scholars think was probably an addition). Now, even though both Genesis 38 and 39 use the name 'YHWH', there is an important difference in the *way* they use it. If you were to remove all of the verses in Genesis 39 that mention YHWH, you would still have a logical and complete story. The main change to the story would be that it would no longer attribute Joseph's success to YHWH's presence with him. If, however, you were to remove from Genesis 38 the two verses that mention YHWH (Gen. 38.7 and 10), the story wouldn't make sense anymore. Try it and see! Important information would be missing from the beginning of the story, so that it no longer flows. All of this evidence (plus one or two other factors) lead scholars to think that Genesis 38 *as a whole* was added later to the story that once ran from Ch 37 directly to Ch 39 and that at the same time, the verses of Genesis 39 that mention YHWH (Gen. 39.2–3, 5, 21–23) were added to the version of Genesis 39 that was already there. (Probably the 'resumption' in verse 1 was added also.) Now, the implication of this kind of reading is that we should perhaps be a little wary about drawing too many theological conclusions from the fact that YHWH is present with Joseph in Genesis 39 and not elsewhere. There are many possible reasons for adding references to YHWH at this stage and not elsewhere *that have little or nothing to do with theology about Joseph and YHWH's relationship.*

If we wanted to, we could go on and ask *why* a later author, editor or storyteller would choose to add the extra verses in Genesis 39. It is important to note that any conclusion we reached could be no more than hypothetical, but perhaps we would want to try anyway. I'm going to give it a shot. These verses remind me of another Genesis story. If you read *Abraham: A journey,* you might remember reading part of the Isaac story from Genesis 26 in the last chapter of the book. Isaac's story is quite brief, and one of its features is that Isaac tends to repeat many of the things his father, Abraham, had previously done. Genesis 26 is like a mosaic of Abraham stories, but attributed to Isaac. At the beginning and end of the chapter are some added verses – a bit like the verses we think may have been added to Genesis 39. In fact, very alike! The function of these verses in Genesis 26 is to transmit the promises that God had previously made to Abraham to his son Isaac. God makes covenants with Abraham at the beginning of his story, but doesn't make further covenants with Abraham's son and grandson – instead there are passages where the original covenant promises are transferred to them.

One interesting thing about the transfer of promises from Abraham to Isaac in Genesis 26.3–5 and 24 is that the story copies elements from stories in which royal promises are transferred from

King David to his descendants in the book of Kings. I talked about this in *Abraham: A journey*. Some of those elements are right at home in the book of Kings, but don't really belong in Genesis. What I notice about the added verses in Genesis 39 is that they also have some of these distinctive elements. So, for example, in both Genesis 26 and 39, we read that YHWH promises to be (or is) 'with' the ancestor *and* this divine presence is connected with blessing. In both cases, non-Israelites (Abimelech in Genesis 26 and Potiphar and possibly also the chief jailer in Genesis 39) *see* that YHWH is with the ancestor. Additionally, in both places, YHWH blesses or promises to bless a character for 'the sake of' somebody else. Each of these elements is highly distinctive – you won't find anything similar anywhere else in Genesis, either all together or individually. What I make of all this is that somebody wanted to add verses to Genesis 39 that would imply that God's covenant promises, originally made to Abraham, were now being extended to Joseph just as they had previously been extended to Isaac.

Now, I did promise you that we would look at Genesis 38, and we should do that now. On the surface, Genesis 38 seems to tell a completely separate (even slightly random) story about Joseph's elder brother Judah. In the story, Judah has married and has three sons. The eldest son, Er, marries a woman called Tamar, but he is wicked and YHWH puts him to death before they have had any children. Israel's law about levirate marriage (see Deut. 25.5–10) required the next eldest son to marry his brother's widow in such circumstances, so that they can together have a child 'for' the woman's dead husband. So Judah's middle son, Onan, has to marry Tamar, but when he comes to consummate the marriage, he spills his seed on the ground (practises *coitus interruptus*) because he knows the child will be his brother's and not his own, so YHWH puts him to death also. Perhaps unsurprisingly, under the circumstances, Judah becomes worried for the life of his third son and refuses to give Shelah to Tamar in marriage. You probably know what happens from here. Tamar, who realizes that Judah has not given her his third son as he ought to have done, dresses up as a prostitute and waits on the side of the road in order to seduce Judah. As her payment, she keeps his signet, cord and staff as a pledge. Three months later, word comes to Judah that Tamar has been 'playing the harlot' and is pregnant. Judah sends for Tamar so that she can be burned, but Tamar sends in response the signet, cord and staff with a message that their owner is also the man who made her pregnant. Judah acknowledges them as his (thus confirming his role in her pregnancy) and says, 'She is more in the right than I, because I did not give her to my son Shelah.'

Now, it is extremely interesting that there should be a story about Judah so close to Genesis 39 and therefore to the transfer of the promises to Joseph that I've argued has been added to it. Judah is Joseph's most likely rival to succeed Jacob as the 'chosen' son. He is not Jacob's firstborn – in fact Judah has three elder brothers – but they all do things to disqualify themselves from the honour. Reuben disqualifies himself as Jacob's successor when he sleeps with Jacob's concubine (Gen. 49.4), and Simeon and Levi achieve the same with their violent response to the sexual abuse of Dinah (Gen. 49.5–7). Judah is next in line. In the final chapter of *this* book, we will see that Genesis 49 contains a lengthy record of the blessings spoken by Jacob over his twelve sons shortly before his death. Most of the blessings are quite short, and some, including those for his three eldest sons, don't look much like blessings at all. The blessings for *both* Judah and Joseph, however, are long, and each gives the impression of being the blessing due to the chosen son (Gen. 49.8–12 [Judah], 22–26 [Joseph]). What we know from the rest of the biblical record, of course, is that it is Judah (the Southern Kingdom) that becomes God's special chosen kingdom. Curiously, Judah's blessing even implies that Judah overshadows and even *displaces* Joseph – Genesis 49.8 reads, 'Judah, your brothers shall praise you; your hand shall be on the neck of your enemies; your father's sons shall bow down before you.' You will remember, of course, that it was Joseph, and not Judah, who dreamt of his brothers bowing down before him in Genesis 37. There seems to be evidence of quite a tussle going on between (authorial) supporters of Joseph (the north) and Judah (the south)!

I've already suggested that the added verses in Genesis 39 may have been put there by a supporter of Joseph, who wanted to resist Judah's displacement of Joseph in the story. One possibility is that the same person added Genesis 38 so that readers could compare Judah and Joseph in their two 'seduction' stories – Judah's seduction by Tamar and Joseph's by Mrs Potiphar. At first blush, Judah comes off the poorer in the comparison – he fails in his levirate duty to his eldest son, he visits a prostitute and he is exposed as a hypocrite when he threatens to burn Tamar for 'playing the whore'. Joseph arguably fares better – he foils Mrs Potiphar's attempted seduction of him, keeping his righteousness intact, even if he then winds up in jail.

If you dig a little deeper, however, the relative virtues of the two stories becomes a little less clear. There is a hint in Genesis 38 that Judah is transformed by his interactions with Tamar. Once he discovers that he himself had been the man who made her pregnant, and once he is forced to confront his own failure to give his youngest son to Tamar pursuant to the levirate laws, he demonstrates striking remorse. He tells Tamar (a mere Canaanite woman) that she is 'more in the right' than he (Gen. 38.26), because she took steps to ensure that his eldest son, Er, would be succeeded by a son when he himself, the boy's father and a Hebrew, did not. It is to this story that readers of Genesis look when they want to understand how the Judah of Genesis 37 who wanted to profit from his brother Joseph's death becomes the Judah who takes on the mantle of wise leader of the brothers later on in the story. Joseph, however, demonstrates no such transformation. Yes, he manages to avoid sexual congress with Mrs Potiphar, but he goes on behaving afterwards in precisely the same manner that he had before, becoming the new favourite of the next authority figure in his life and relating to those inferior to him only when advantageous to him to do so.

I'm afraid that this has been a rather lengthy explanation of a vertical, or 'diachronic', reading of Genesis 39! What it suggests is that the references to YHWH, and YHWH's presence with Joseph in Genesis 39 may not be connected to theology (the question of how God acts in the story) at all, but may be more political in nature – related to the vexed question of whether Judah or Joseph is to be 'chosen' as Jacob's heir. The added chapter and verses may have been the work of a Joseph/northern kingdom supporter, jockeying to support a favourite ancestor, or perhaps to unsettle an already dominant 'Judah tradition'.

I wonder how you feel about the results of this diachronic reading? Are you disappointed by the idea that the references to YHWH in Genesis 39, and the account of YHWH's influence on Joseph's circumstances, may not best be understood as communicating anything about the nature of God, or about the mode of God's relating with humans? Or do you find the idea of a political dimension to the story interesting, or even exciting? Synchronic and diachronic approaches are ways of reading that scholars have developed to help them 'draw out' the meaning of text. Some scholars prefer synchronic methods and use them exclusively. Others prefer diachronic methods and use them exclusively. The majority, however, use both methods because they are convinced that these different methods can help to shine the most light on Scripture's meaning when they are used together. That means that you are welcome to adopt either, or both, of the readings that I've outlined. If you are interested by both, how do the two look when they are held together? Do they tell you more about the meaning of the passage than just one alone?

Joseph in jail

So we (finally!) come to the end of our reading of Genesis 39. Joseph is in jail, but already he has won the confidence of his jailer and been put in charge of his fellow prisoners. On the surface, he is doing well – growing in strength and influence and moving toward the centre of Egyptian power: Pharaoh himself. What I have tried to do in this chapter, however, is to focus our attention on Joseph's vulnerability below the façade of success, and I have suggested that resilience has got more to do with addressing injuries and hurts than it has to do with sailing on as if nothing has happened. I've also argued that resilience has more to do with resolving hurts and injuries than it has with identifying excessively with one's own vulnerabilities and wounds. So, if resilience is about neither 'just getting on with it' nor 'adopting professional victimhood', what is it about? In the next chapter, we will think more about what resilience *is* and how to build it. *And* we'll find out what happens to Joseph next.

3

The Egyptian

GENESIS 40—41

So Pharaoh said to Joseph, 'Since God has shown you all this, there is no one so discerning and wise as you. You shall be over my house, and all my people shall order themselves as you command; only with regard to the throne will I be greater than you.' And Pharaoh said to Joseph, 'See, I have set you over all the land of Egypt.' Removing his signet ring from his hand, Pharaoh put it on Joseph's hand; he arrayed him in garments of fine linen, and put a gold chain around his neck. He had him ride in the chariot of his second-in-command; and they cried out in front of him, 'Bow the knee!' Thus he set him over all the land of Egypt. (Gen. 41.39–43)

Have you ever experienced something either so challenging or so dreadful that you had to change your conception of who you are just to keep going? Let me give you a couple of examples while you're thinking about your answer to that question. When a twin dies, the remaining twin has to build a new identity. He or she is no longer one of a pair, but a single person (and also a single person who has sustained a great loss). The surviving twin cannot go on as if nothing has changed, but must adjust to a new identity. Of course, any death may have a similar, if less dramatic, effect on the identity of people closest to the deceased person – the survivors may no longer be mothers, or uncles, or brothers or grandparents, for example. Part of adjusting to the loss is an adjustment to one's own identity. Marriage is another experience that leads to an identity change. When one marries for the first time, one becomes half of a pair instead of a single person. There are lots of changes to navigate (many joyful!) but part of the experience is adjusting to a new (corporate) identity. At the other end of marriage, divorce or the death of a spouse again requires readjustment to singleness.

I have lived through experiences like these at least two or three times. Two of them related to illness, and I'll tell the story of one of those times now. I've already referred to the fact that I lived with Chronic Fatigue Syndrome (CFS), or ME, for nearly the first two decades of my working life. Getting a diagnosis and adjusting to my new limitations took many years. I also had to come to terms with the fact that I was now a 'sick person'. Before ME, I'd had the (perhaps slightly odd) idea that I was a 'wash and wear' person. I wasn't especially high maintenance (in my own mind, anyway!) and I had lots of energy and didn't seem to get sick too often. But ME changed a lot of things. I had to husband my energy very carefully and say 'no' a great deal. I had to let people down fairly regularly, when even my conservative assessment of what I might be able to manage turned out to be unrealistic. I also had to take a back seat professionally at a time when most people are consolidating themselves in a career and looking for advancement, and I felt exhausted, lethargic and purposeless much of the time. All of these things made a huge change to my self-perception, but perhaps the most significant thing was that I no longer felt 'useful'. Instead of doing things for myself and other people, I was now someone who had to rely on other people to do things for me. I felt like a dead weight.

I had to work extremely hard to find a sense of identity that had some meaning for me. In fact, the whole concept of 'meaning' became far more important than it had ever been before. I needed to find some kind of meaning in my new limitations and suffering, and I had to find value in the limited things I was still able to *do*. I also realized that I had to build an identity for myself that was about more than just the fact that I was sick. During the worst of it, I was living in a university residential college, gradually cutting down the handful of hours I felt able to teach each week. Even so, being in the college was a boon in a number of ways. There were people and companionship just outside my door. I didn't have to cook for myself. But perhaps the best thing was that the college had a chapel. I could maintain a relatively disciplined life of prayer, both alone and with others. I came to love and value the daily office, and I practiced meditation and taught it to staff and students. I can remember going to see the Principal of the College (who was a priest) and putting a fairly extraordinary proposal to him. I suggested that I take on the identity of 'college hermit'. I argued that it would be of benefit to the college to have a resident who wasn't *busy doing things*, but who had space to 'be' and 'pray'. Looking back, I'd have to say that he received this highly unusual (okay, strange) proposal with grace – at the same time as making it pretty clear that he saw right through it. He and I both knew that I needed an identity that would give me a sense of usefulness and of meaning, and he allowed me the space to create it, at least in my own mind.

Illness is one of the experiences that can require the building of a new identity. 'Cancer survivor' is one such identity – as a person who has experienced considerable pain and dis-ease, and who has faced the possibility of death, adopts markers such as strength, courage, healthfulness, positivity, vitality, vegetarianism or spirituality as central to their new identity post-cancer. Hospital chaplains know the importance of developing a new, or adjusted, sense of identity after the disorientating experience of serious illness – and of the importance of encouraging patients who are in their care (and their families) to imagine ways into new futures and new identities.

In this chapter we will be thinking further about this process of building a new identity after a crisis (whether joyful or disastrous), and the central role it plays in developing resilience. If you have thought of an example or two from your own life, you should hold them in your mind as we read our way through Chapters 40 and 41 of Genesis, following Joseph on his path to power in Egypt. We'll see that Joseph adopts this principle of adapting one's identity wholeheartedly – he responds to the crisis of his trafficking to Egypt, his enslavement and his imprisonment in an Egyptian prison by becoming thoroughly Egyptian. Arguably, he becomes more Egyptian than the Egyptians! Does it work for him? Let's see.

The Dreamer becomes the Dream Whisperer

We find Joseph at the beginning of Genesis 40 in the prison into which he'd been banished after the debacle with Mrs Potiphar. You might remember that Joseph had been given special responsibilities in the prison. The chief jailer had committed all the prisoners into Joseph's care, and YHWH had caused Joseph to prosper, whatever he did. At the beginning of Chapter 40, Joseph is called upon to serve two new prisoners – two of Pharaoh's chief functionaries, a cupbearer and a baker, whose crime has been to offend Pharaoh. This time it is not Joseph who dreams, but his two new charges. They appear before Joseph one morning looking downcast because they have no one to interpret their dreams. Joseph says to them something a little odd: 'Do not interpretations belong to God? Please tell them to me.' What exactly is Joseph saying here? Is he claiming some special divine agency, or is he just trying to have it both ways – appearing pious but also taking the opportunity to step in and be the saviour?

In any event, the two are sufficiently encouraged by this ambiguous invitation to tell Joseph their dreams. Each has dreamed a dream corresponding to his former employment. The chief cupbearer has dreamed of three branches that bud and grow fruit, which the cupbearer presses into Pharaoh's cup. Joseph tells him that the three branches represent three days, and that after three days, Pharaoh will 'lift up' the cupbearer's head and restore him to his former role.

In the light of this positive interpretation, Joseph sees the opportunity to put in a good word for himself. He tells the cupbearer that he has been stolen 'from the land of the Hebrews' and wrongly imprisoned and asks the cupbearer to speak on his behalf once he has Pharaoh's ear again. Meanwhile, the chief baker, also encouraged by the favourable interpretation, tells Joseph his dream also: he has three baskets of baked goods for Pharaoh on his head, but birds come and eat the cakes from the baskets. This time, the interpretation is unfavourable. Again, says Joseph, the baskets represent three days, indicating that within three days Pharaoh will 'lift up' the head of his former employee – but this time Pharaoh will lift the baker's head right off his shoulders! The pun is clearly there in the Hebrew. Pharaoh will hang the baker by his neck from a pole, and birds will eat his flesh.

It all comes about exactly as Joseph has foretold. The third day, which happens to be a feast day for Pharaoh's birthday, arrives, and Pharaoh lifts up both heads, restoring the chief cupbearer to his former duties, but hanging the chief baker, just as Joseph had predicted. Joseph's initial foray into the interpretation of dreams has been remarkably successful.

What are we to make of the accuracy of Joseph's interpretations? Does it suggest that Joseph is enjoying divine favour? (In other words, have the interpretations been given to him by God?) Or could any intelligent person have predicted this outcome or one like it? We will need to read on to get a sense about this. The only real disappointment for Joseph is that the cupbearer completely forgets Joseph and Joseph's request. He says nothing of Joseph to Pharaoh, and so Joseph continues to languish in jail for another two years. Incidentally, we will learn in Genesis 41.46 that Joseph is 30 years old when he finally leaves jail and enters Pharaoh's service. He had been only 17 years old when his brothers sold him to the Ishmaelite (sorry, Midianite) traders, so a full 13 years pass between Joseph's original trafficking and his final release from jail! You may not have had a sense of that length of time passing from the narrative, but it seems that Joseph's ordeal is extremely protracted.

Resilience in the short and long terms

So far in this book I have talked about resilience in terms of the ability to 'bounce back' from crises or setbacks. We often think of resilience in this way – a process of recovering and coming back from single, brief disasters. A 13-year experience of enslavement and imprisonment, however, could not be described as a 'single, brief disaster' in anybody's language. The image of 'bouncing back' doesn't really work very well in the context of such a protracted trauma. Instead, what is needed is an ability to adjust and adapt so that a person can develop a response to the situation that is sustainable over an extended period. Apparently, this was something that Joseph was able to cultivate. The story doesn't give us a lot of detail, but we know that Joseph survived his predicament for a long time, and that when the opportunity to free himself came, he was able to grasp it (even if he had to wait another two years before his plans bore fruit).

That begs the question of what is really meant by 'resilience', so it is time now to look at resilience in a slightly deeper way. The real problem with defining resilience is that there are just about as many definitions as there are practitioners in the field. The previously mentioned American Psychological Associations definition, which talks about the ability to 'bounce back', is perhaps the one that is most often referenced, but in truth there are many approaches to defining resilience. One influential feature of the APA definition, and others like it, is the idea that resilience is not a character trait that one is either born with or not, but a 'process' that one can learn and develop. This is important because it means that resilience can be viewed as a therapeutic tool to be cultivated by individuals and by communities, and that idea makes resilience worth talking about and studying.

So, resilience is typically thought of as a 'process', and many, or most, definitions break the process down into a number of individual 'factors' that individuals or communities can cultivate. Some commentators on resilience identify a relatively small number of factors – say, three – while others compile long lists of ten or more, while still others are content to promote a single 'factor' or 'mechanism'. These last are probably least helpful for individuals because they tend to roll a number of ideas up into a single ball. The lengthy lists can be instructive because they identify so many individual ideas and approaches. For example, Stephen M. Southwick and Dennis Charney nominate ten key 'factors' for resilience: realistic optimism; facing fear; moral compass; religion and spirituality; social support; resilient role models; physical fitness; brain fitness; cognitive and emotional flexibility and meaning and purpose. (See the list of Further Reading at the back of this book.)The APA site to which I directed you to in Chapter One also includes an extensive list of factors. Most of these factors are relatively self-explanatory and perhaps also relatively predictable. The idea is that if you work on each of these things, or a substantial number of them, you will increase your overall resilience.

I'll refer to some of these factors from time to time, but I won't dwell on them. You may be pleased to hear, for example, that while I'm entirely in favour of physical fitness and convinced of the contribution it can make to personal resilience, I won't be setting you a daily exercise target! Instead, I want to focus on a definition that identifies slightly more complicated or compound 'factors'. Whitehead and Whitehead, in a 2016 study (that, again, I'll reference for you later) identify three factors (all conveniently beginning with the letter 'r') that can be developed by individuals or communities seeking to build their resilience: these are 'reframing', 'recruitability' and 'resolve'. By 'reframing', they mean a form of flexibility which allows an individual or group to reinterpret negative experiences. By 'recruitability', they mean the capacity to build connections with other people. By 'resolve', they mean the element of determination that propels a person or community to keep on going in the face of stresses, shocks and setbacks. Over the next chapters, I will be exploring these three factors in some detail as we read the rest of Joseph's story together.

In this chapter our focus will be on 'reframing'. If you look back to the beginning of this chapter, you'll be reminded that I started out by asking you whether you've ever had the experience of needing to make adjustments to your sense of identity following a crisis (either disastrous or joyful). This is an important part of what Whitehead and Whitehead mean by 'reframing'. 'Reframing' is about telling a story – the story of your own life – in a new way. It may literally involve constructing a new 'frame' around the story you've always told about yourself, or it might mean telling your story with a new emphasis, or from a new perspective, or with a completely new ending. Do you ever think about your life as a story? I did, even before I knew very much of the theory of stories or understood how telling stories could be therapeutic. I used to wonder what kind of story it was that I was living. Would it prove to be a comedy or even a romance? For the longest time I feared that my life might take on the shape of tragedy, or even that I would one day discover that I had been living a prolonged and dramatic farce. Even if we have an idea about the shape of our story right now, we never know when a dramatic turn of events might suddenly or comprehensively reshape our future. 'Reframing' is about being able to adjust and adapt the way you tell your story so that you can incorporate the new developments into the old reality with both congruence and integrity, and so that you can face new circumstances in your future.

I've already talked about my experience of having to re-adjust my identity or, in other words, 'retell my story' when I developed ME. I had another such experience when I finally overcame ME and became 'well' again. After having lived for more than a decade (actually, closer to two) as a 'sick' person, I had to find a new identity for myself (tell a new life story) all over again when I got well. (In truth, this process of reframing never really stops, as we'll see below.) Having adapted to my limitations, I needed to learn to live without them once more. Of course, this was a far more joyful transition than the earlier experience had been, but it was in some ways no less difficult – and ten years on, I'm still not sure I've completely achieved it.

Let me say a little more about that. When I was ill, I came to find my meaning or purpose largely through spirituality and the disciplines of worship, prayer and meditation. These were the 'meaning-making' activities that I was still able, despite my limited capacities, to engage in. You'll remember that the identity of 'hermit' was one that resonated with me. Once I was well again, I had far fewer limitations; I could engage in any number of activities that might help me to feel a sense of meaning, purpose or 'usefulness'. I re-engaged in full-time work, and I wrote a doctoral thesis. I started exercising again, volunteered and engaged in a newly active social life. But now the problem was different – what new spiritual practice or identity would I adopt to support and complement my newly rich and active life? The contemplative life came relatively easily to me, and in many ways my spirituality has been informed and shaped by suffering and loss. Who would I be as a Christian and a spiritual person once much of what I had lost had been restored? It makes me think of the challenges that Job's 'happy ending' must have raised for him, and of the complaint of the 'ex-leper' in Monty Python's *Life of Brian* that he had lost not only his identity but also his income and livelihood! The problem was 'compounded' when I suddenly and very unexpectedly found a husband and moved to a new country to marry him. How would I incorporate the identities of 'married person' (after nearly 50 years of single life) and 'Brit' (after nearly 50 years of life as an Antipodean) into my new identity? I'm still not entirely sure I've found the answer here either!

The therapeutic power of stories

The power of stories, and their capacity to be therapeutic, is not always fully appreciated. One field of study in which the power of stories *has* been fully grasped is gerontology. Gerontology deals with the phenomenon of aging. Aging can, for many people, be experienced as a slow, extended trauma, as body and mind gradually disintegrate over time and as a person's horizon seems, imperceptibly, to constrict. In this scenario, stories – and in particular, the re-framing of stories – can be powerful. Just as I needed to build an identity for myself (or tell a story about myself) that instilled in me a sense of meaning and purpose during the years when I lived with ME (and needed to do it all over again when I recovered), so the experience of aging can create a compelling need for stories that bring meaning and purpose to lives that might otherwise seem to be defined by increasing lack or failure. One gerontologist who works with stories in this way is a pastor called William L. Randall. He argues that what is most needed for building resilience in later life is 'a good, strong story'. What he means by 'a good, strong story' is one that stretches out beyond ourselves, and beyond our families and communities, to engage generations who lived many years before us and others who will live many years after we are gone. He writes, 'A good strong story reaches out—in humility and awe—to something grander than ourselves, to a vaster narrative than that of our own little self, to [...] the "transcendent horizon of the life story".' In other words, our life story should be bigger than ourselves and our personal experience. If we are able to introduce a sense of the cosmic (and a good splash of irony, suggests Randall) and engage with a larger reality, we are more likely to find a story that will sustain us and build resilience within us.

This is part of the reason why religious faith and practice are often recognized (even by non-religious types) as factors that can help to increase and sustain resilience. It is also, I believe, why engaging with biblical stories and telling our own stories in the shape of those ancient stories, can be so helpful for us in building our own resilience levels. Many biblical stories are 'resilient' themselves, and by 'living into' them and taking on their contours, we reach out to something grander than ourselves, and we expand our horizons to comprehend the transcendent. So perhaps we should get back to Joseph.

Joseph does some reframing

When we begin to read Genesis 41, we discover that Chapter 40 was really just an extended introduction to this absolutely pivotal story. Everything that happens here has been set up by the account of Joseph's encounter with the cupbearer and baker. At the beginning of Chapter 41, we learn that Joseph has languished an extra two years in Pharaoh's prison. His fortunes, however, are finally about to change. This time, it is Pharaoh who dreams. His dreams are more complicated than those of his cupbearer and baker. First, Pharaoh dreams that seven sleek and plump cows come up out of the Nile and feed on its banks. Then seven thin and ugly cows come out, and they eat the fat cows. In his second dream, Pharaoh dreams that seven plump ears of grain are growing on a single stalk. Then a further seven ears sprout after them. They are 'thin and blighted by the east wind'. The last seven ears swallow up the first plump ears. Pharaoh is troubled by these dreams, but even though he consults all of the magicians of Egypt and all of Egypt's wise men, no one can interpret them for him.

Finally, the chief cupbearer remembers the Hebrew who had interpreted dreams for himself and the baker. He tells Pharaoh the story, explaining that their fates had been revealed exactly as Joseph had predicted. Pharaoh, suitably impressed, summons Joseph, who is brought before him. A small detail might be missed here if we are not attentive. Genesis 41.14 notes in passing that before Joseph appears before Pharaoh, he changes his clothes and cuts his hair. Now, you probably think that these are obvious things for a prisoner to do before meeting the king. Of course you're right, but here there is an extra significance about Joseph's haircut. Egyptians were distinctive in their context in that they – and most particularly, Egyptian priests – wore their hair short. We need to acknowledge the possibility here that Joseph is deliberately setting out to look Egyptian, and possibly also deliberately setting out to look like an Egyptian priest.

Pharaoh tells Joseph that he understands that Joseph can interpret dreams and asks him if he will interpret his dreams. Joseph's response is quite similar to his strange response to the chief cup-bearer and baker. The NRSV translates Joseph's reply, 'It is not I. God will give Pharaoh a favourable answer. (Genesis 41:16)' In fact, the Hebrew here is a little complicated, so that Joseph's meaning is not entirely clear, but it appears that Joseph replies piously, saying, in essence, that interpretation belongs to God. (Note, however, that the name for God that is used here is 'Elohim' and not YHWH as in Genesis 39.) In any event, Pharaoh seems satisfied, and so he tells Joseph his dreams.

It is at this point that Lloyd-Weber and Rice present us with the stand-out line of their musical: Joseph sings, 'The things you saw in your pyjamas/ were a long-range forecast for your farmers'. More prosaically described, Joseph tells Pharaoh that his two dreams are one and the same. God has used the two dreams to tell Pharaoh what He would do in Egypt over the next 14 years. The first seven years would be good years – years of plenty – but they would be followed by seven lean years – years of famine – that would 'eat up' all of the abundance of the good years. By doubling the dreams, Joseph tells Pharaoh, God has indicated that the thing is fixed and that it will come about soon. (Incidentally, in the Hebrew language, repetition is a tactic for adding emphasis and intensity.)

Despite all of his pious protestations that interpretation belongs to God, Joseph doesn't stop just with interpreting Pharaoh's dreams, but goes on to tell Pharaoh how to respond to the dreams and what to do. What he goes on to say is bold for a non-Egyptian who has just been brought out of Pharaoh's prison:

> Now therefore let Pharaoh select a man who is discerning and wise, and set him over the land of Egypt. Let Pharaoh proceed to appoint overseers over the land, and take one-fifth of the produce of the land of Egypt during the seven plenteous years. Let them gather all the food of these good years that are coming, and lay up grain under the authority of Pharaoh for food in the cities, and let them keep it. That food shall be a reserve for the land against the seven years of famine that are to befall the land of Egypt, so that the land may not perish through the famine. (Gen. 41.33–36)

Does Joseph have himself in mind in making this proposal? It is impossible to tell from the text (in the musical there is a humorous interlude in which Pharaoh and his courtiers rush around the stage, desperately looking for such a discerning and wise person, only to realise eventually that Joseph is standing right in front of them), but his words certainly fix Joseph in Pharaoh's mind. Pharaoh is impressed with Joseph. He says to his servants, 'Can we find anyone else like this – one in whom is the spirit of God?' Then Pharaoh goes on to make an arrangement with Joseph that is very like the arrangements that Potiphar and the chief jailer had previously made with him. Yet again, somebody puts Joseph in charge of everything that he has – his whole house. This time, the person is Pharaoh and all he has – his whole household – is all the land of Egypt. Only the throne Pharaoh holds back from Joseph, as Potiphar had previously held back only the food that he ate.

A number of things are remarkable about this. The foreign slave-prisoner suddenly becomes the second-most important person in all of Egypt. Pharaoh is the only person who exceeds him in influence. Joseph's circumstances are completely turned around.

And yet, what Pharaoh does for Joseph is precisely what Potiphar and the jailer have previously done. Apparently, something about Joseph immediately inspires confidence! It is also remarkable that Pharaoh picks up on Joseph's God talk and matches it. What God is Pharaoh speaking of? Are Joseph and Pharaoh speaking of the same God, or does the generic name 'God' allow both to speak of his own God?

Yes, God is in the story here. But note that God is present in a different way than was the case in Genesis 39. Do you remember that in Joseph's dealings with both Potiphar and the chief jailer, the narrative stressed that YHWH (God's special name) blessed Joseph and his work, and that YHWH was the cause of Joseph's prosperity and the prosperity that Joseph brought to his master? There are no statements like that in this account of Joseph's new relationship with Pharaoh. Both Joseph and Pharaoh speak of God, but the narrator does not say that God is with Joseph and Pharaoh or that He blesses them. Is God still there with Joseph, behind everything that he does, or is Joseph just very, very good at taking advantage of opportunities that are presented to him?

Let's hold that question in our minds and come back to the story. Pharaoh covers Joseph in glory. He takes off his own signet ring and puts it on Joseph's finger. He dresses Joseph in a fine linen robe and puts a gold chain around his neck. Pharaoh causes Joseph to ride in the chariot of his second-in-command and those riding before him cry out 'Bow the knee!' He tells Joseph that without his (Joseph's) consent, no one will 'lift up hand or foot in all the land of Egypt'. Pharaoh even gives Joseph an Egyptian name, Zaphenath-panea, and an Egyptian wife, Asenath, daughter of Potiphera, a priest of the god On. 'Thus Joseph gained authority over the land of Egypt' (Gen. 41.45). Joseph is now, for all intents and purposes, Egyptian. He wears Egyptian clothing and jewellery; he has an Egyptian name; he has an Egyptian wife, and he has short hair, like his Egyptian father-in-law. In other words, Joseph has re-invented himself. You might fairly object that he hasn't done it all himself. But nor has Joseph objected to any of it. He doesn't say to Pharaoh, 'I will do this for you, but I will remain a Hebrew.' As we've already seen, Joseph is good at capitalizing on the opportunities he's given. In short, Joseph makes a change in his identity that will help him to navigate the future. Through his relationship with Pharaoh, his new clothes and his new family, he tells a new story about himself.

Joseph wastes no time in exercising his new authority. He travels around Egypt, gathering up all of the food that is produced during the good years and storing it in warehouses. He collects so much produce from all around the country that he can no longer measure it. During these good years, Joseph and Asenath have two sons. Joseph names the first Manasseh, 'For God has made me forget all my hardship and all my father's house', and the second he names Ephraim, 'For God has made me fruitful in the land of my misfortunes' (Gen. 41.51–52).

I should concede that these are Hebrew, and not Egyptian, names. Quite often in these stories, names and their meanings are important. There is something really quite curious about the etiology (explanation) of the name Manasseh. Manasseh's name recollects Psalm 45, the most feminine of the psalms. The psalmist tells a young woman in the court of her king to 'forget your people and your father's house':

> Hear, O daughter, consider and incline
> your ear;
> forget your people and your father's house,
> and the king will desire your beauty.
> Since he is your lord, bow to him;
> the people of Tyre will seek your favour
> with gifts,
> the richest of the people with all kinds of
> wealth. (Ps. 45.10–13)

Strangely enough, there is a sense here that Joseph is being portrayed as feminine again – as a young woman bowing to her lord the king, whose people will make her wealthy. The psalm even goes on to describe the princess in her chamber, decked in golden robes, and being led to her king in robes of many colours. (Sound familiar?) If Manasseh's name is supposed to relate to Joseph's situation, then the comparison with a young woman being led to the king, to receive the country's wealth, is perhaps not an entirely positive one, and yet, as we will see, it is entirely predictive of what will happen to Joseph.

The abundance lasts for seven years, just as Joseph predicted, and the good years are duly followed by seven years of famine. Thanks to Pharaoh's dream and Joseph's plan, Egypt has food when its neighbours have none. When the Egyptians come to Pharaoh, crying for bread, he sends them to Joseph with an instruction to do whatever he tells them. In response, Joseph opens the storehouses and sells the stored produce to the people and to the hungry foreigners who have come from all around. Joseph is Egypt's saviour!

I wonder whether you noticed an important little word in the last paragraph? Did you notice that Josephs *sells* the produce to the Egyptians? Selling to the *foreigners* makes perfect sense – after all, why shouldn't Egypt profit from its foresight and prudent husbandry? But this food was produced by the Egyptians, and Joseph hadn't bought it from them – he had simply 'taken' or 'gathered' it. Now, the very people who had grown or produced the food are being required to buy it back again. How is this going to play out? We'll have to wait and see.

Reframing Joseph, you and me

In the story as we've read it so far, Joseph has already re-invented himself several times in Egypt. Starting out as the model house servant and winning the confidence of his master, Joseph later becomes the model prisoner/ jail supervisor, winning the confidence of both his jailer and his fellow prisoners. This latest re-invention is the most dramatic, as Joseph adopts the appearance and habits of his new country – even giving one of his children a name that suggests that he has forgotten his heritage and his father's house in order to serve Pharaoh.

It is interesting that many of Joseph's incarnations have brought with them distinctive items of clothing. His initial 'coat with sleeves' represents his status as his father's favourite son (while also having a whiff of 'princess' about it). This coat also becomes the evidence that convinces his father of Joseph's violent demise. Later, his house coat, his slave garb, becomes the evidence that convicts him of attempted seduction of Mrs Potiphar. Now, in this latest incarnation, a robe of fine linen marks Joseph as Pharaoh's anointed assistant, giving the Egyptian people all the evidence they need that Joseph has the authority to requisition their property.

If 'reframing' is to be understood as a factor of resilience, then I think you would have to say that Joseph proves himself to be highly resilient. He survives 13 years as a slave and then a prisoner in a foreign country – and at the end of it all, he is able to take advantage of the opportunities that come his way *and* he is sufficiently flexible and canny to re-invent himself as an Egyptian and make the most of having attracted Pharaoh's attention. He succeeds beyond anybody's expectations. And yet, at each stage there is a core of his personality that remains unchanged. Joseph apparently retains an unshakeable faith in his own worth. The precocious child who sees himself as superior to his older brothers, and who wins the favouritism of their father, continues to win favouritism wherever he goes, and he takes advantage of every opportunity to further himself, even in the face of repeated betrayal. In other words, while Joseph is able to re-invent himself repeatedly, he is also able to retain the core of his personality and his vitality. He is able to bounce back.

As I write this and reflect on Joseph's story, I am acutely aware that my own latest personal re-invention is still a work in progress.

It is now five years since I married, and a little longer since I moved countries. In the last ten years all my most pressing 'problems' have been resolved. I am no longer defined in my mind, in any sense, by illness or by singleness. I have a wonderful husband; I live in one of the most exciting cities in the world, near some of the world's most extraordinary places of worship; I write books (who knew?); some of my efforts at building friendships are beginning to bear fruit; I don't eat *too* much chocolate and sometimes I even exercise. And yet, there are many things I still need to resolve. I need to work out how to hold on to the core of who I am, while being flexible enough to become the person who is living this blessed life and to respond to the opportunities that present themselves. This might not sound to you like a crisis, but I will not be able to live fully into this new life until I have built a new frame around my life story and until I have taken on the wholeness of my new identity. Until those things have happened, I will not know fully who I am as child of God, wife of R., and daughter, sister, aunt, godmother and friend of loved people living far away.

There is yet another piece of re-framing that is looming not too far away on my horizon. As I write these words, R., who is a little older than me, will shortly be retiring. He is looking forward to retirement, which he hopes will give him lots more time to do things that he really wants to do, especially writing. He has some apprehension about this life change, however, and fairly so. R. has been in the same job for decades. It has been a highly stimulating and creative and demanding role, which has brought him in contact with some extraordinarily stimulating and creative and demanding people, and it has had an immeasurable impact upon his construction of his identity. Not only the role, but also the institution in which he has performed it, have become part of who he is. Detaching himself from all of that and 're-framing' his identity to that of a retired person is likely to prove an enormous challenge. Cleverly, he has arranged to go on extended retreat just at the time of the transition. (He's telling friends that he's going to be silent for 35 days because he likes to hear them laugh!) He will have a spiritual guide available to him for an hour every day to encourage and walk alongside him as he negotiates this treacherous transition and as he embarks on the journey of identifying a new identity and a new vocation. During R.'s retreat, which will follow the Ignatian pattern, he will be guided through the gospel stories of Christ's life, passion and resurrection. At each stage he will be invited to see himself in these stories, finding links between them and his own, and discerning God's will for him through the process.

The process is not unlike the approach I'm trying to model for you in this book. It assumes the biblical stories to be transforming and life-affirming, and it encourages us to tell our own stories in the shape of those stories. This approach is a highly effective way of building resilience. First and foremost, it is of God. But there are any number of other reasons. Stories, in addition to the other things I've already said about them, can be highly *flexible*, and flexibility, along with meaning, is at the heart of resilience. Stories can be added to and can change direction as they go along. A single new detail or nuance can be all it takes to shift the entire feeling of a story. Stories are also rather like diamonds in that they look different depending on where you're standing (or what the light is like, or what you had for breakfast). They also look different over time. You might have had the experience of revisiting a favourite story – biblical or not – after having not read it for a time and discovering entirely new things in it, or finding that it seems to 'mean' the opposite of what you had always understood its meaning to be. Stories reflect the light, you see, and by this, I mean the light that you, the reader, shine upon them. Whereas the meaning of a doctrinal tract or a technical manual, for example, will have meaning that is relatively fixed, the meaning of a story can be elusive and changeable, depending upon what we bring to it. When you bring the *flexibility* of story together with the *meaning* of Scripture, you have a powerful agent for resilience building.

Resilience and biblical storytelling

There are certainly many biblical stories in both testaments that you could read as accounts of the lives of resilient characters. Joseph is arguably one of those. However, the Scriptures have much more to share with us in terms of resilience modelling, and especially the modelling of reframing, than just individual stories. The entire Bible, in fact, is a great big collection of reframing exercises! I'm going to focus on the Old Testament (OT) more generally for a bit here, although a lot of what I'll have to say concerns the role of Genesis in the larger biblical story and also the function that the Joseph story performs in that context.

So far in this chapter, I've concentrated on the life stories of individuals and the need for you and me to reframe our stories as we encounter traumatic or otherwise dramatic events. Pretty much everything I've said, however, applies equally to groups of people, like nations or tribes. It is easy for us to forget that our Scriptures are, at their most very basic, collective exercises in identity creation and management. Just as *we* must, the OT writers wrote stories to help construct Israel's identity as the chosen people of God – and to reconstruct or reframe that identity when disaster struck as, I'm afraid, it did fairly often. Luckily for us, their methods of reframing the story of Israel can be helpful as models, *and* they are also not too difficult to reconstruct, because ancient Israelite scribes tended to conserve most of what was written about God and therefore kept the old along with the new (Matthew 13:52). That is why when we read OT books, and especially the first five that comprise the Torah, we can become aware of passages in different places – or even in the same place – that say different things about Israel's law and history. The old, unreframed story is included together with the new. So, to give you an example, Genesis 1 is probably a later, reframed account of God's creation that sits right alongside Genesis 2. Whereas Genesis 2 is the particular story of an immanent, personal God who creates the individual humans who become the ancestors of the nation of Israel, Genesis 1 is a universalist story of a transcendent God who creates the world and everything in it, including all peoples. It 'reaches out to the transcendent horizons of the world', to refer back to Randall's work on ageing. These two very different models of God-in-creation are reflected later in the OT in different strands of the story that focus their attention either on the God of Israel or the God of all the nations.

The primary disaster event that prompted reframing in the OT was the destruction of Jerusalem and the exile of Judah in Babylon. If you think about how the West has had to rethink its identity and relationship with the East following 9/11, you will *begin* to have some idea of what Judah was dealing with. There are interesting parallels because in each case it had been thought that the city in question – Jerusalem, on the one hand, and New York, on the other – would never be vulnerable to attack. What happened to New York had such impact because it was *unthinkable*. The impact of the *unthinkable* happening to Jerusalem was similarly enormous. The Judeans had built their identity on being God's chosen people, whom God would always bless and protect. What did it mean that this God, YHWH, had now allowed them to be defeated? Was YHWH weaker than the gods of the Babylonians, or had God simply given up on them? This was a pressing problem for the exiled Judeans. We can see from what was written during that period, however, that they came up with an ingenious bit of reframing that avoided having to reach either of those unpalatable conclusions. YHWH was neither weak nor fickle – rather, YHWH was strong and faithful and had used the Babylonians to punish the Judeans for their failure to keep YHWH's Torah. YHWH wasn't just the weak, local God of a small nation; YHWH was the God and Creator of the entire world and of *all* nations, who could use mighty empires like Babylon to administer necessary punishment to beloved, chosen Judah. (Are you starting to see how Genesis 1 fits into the picture now?) In all likelihood, the exiled Judeans were influenced by everything they saw in the sophisticated Babylon and probably also by their encounter there with the universalist Persian god Ahura Mazda.

For a time, this reframing of YHWH proved to be a highly effective and resilient strategy. It allowed the exiles to believe that YHWH would eventually return them to their land and renew the covenant relationship. And, sure enough, that is exactly what happened. In due course, the Persian Empire succeeded Babylon, and the Judeans, along with other exiled peoples, were allowed to return to their homes. Unfortunately for the Judeans, it wasn't the homecoming they had dreamt of and longed for. Instead of the land of milk and honey of their imaginations, they discovered what seemed like a dusty backwater in comparison with Babylon's bright lights and sophistication. Worse, the poorer, lower-class Judeans who hadn't been taken into exile had re-established themselves in the homes and fields of the exiles. There were no city walls, there was no temple and as time went on, it became more and more apparent that there wouldn't be another Davidic king either. It wasn't long before tensions between the returners and those who'd never left festered and grew, and major identity crises overtook both groups, as they jostled to be recognized as the true Israel and the chosen nation.

In the midst of all of this, it became apparent to the returners that the reframing that had served them so well in exile in Babylon wouldn't really work in this new, disillusioned reality. A theology of punishment did nothing to help the returners move into the future. (It doesn't work *at all* today either, as the holocaust brought home all too graphically.) The reality was, the returners realized, that they were a stiff-necked people and unable to have confidence in their own ability to keep God's Torah in the long term. They had also, if they were honest with themselves, to realize that they lacked confidence in the promises God had made to them. When would the next one be broken, and how long would it be until they next found themselves being picked up by the scruff of the neck and cast out of their land and their chosen status? The problem with the covenant theology they'd developed was that it could all too easily be brought to an end when one side or the other failed to keep its side of the bargain. A further reframing exercise was needed. So that's what they did. The returners re-imagined their covenant theology, so that the covenant could survive (and the people could remain in the land) even when things went wrong. The change required quite a lot of rethinking. The first thing was to make actions, both good and bad, the responsibility of individuals rather than of the community. That way, when the Torah was breached, the culprits could be excommunicated (or 'cut off') from the community, which could carry on unaffected in covenant terms. As well as restricting punishment to a specific group of people, punishment was also restricted in time; whereas previously, punishment had been understood to extend to the third or fourth generation of the offender (e.g. Exod. 20.5–6; Deut. 5.9–10), now it would be restricted to the offender themselves (e.g. Deut. 7.9–11; Ezekiel 18). Instead of the exile being the result of the actions of King Manasseh (three or four generations prior), as the previous reframing had determined (2 Kgs. 24.1–4), it was the result of the actions of *all* the people immediately prior to the attack on Jerusalem (2 Chr. 36.15–21).

Have you ever done the exercise of reading the Bible from beginning to end? If you have (and you made it all the way through Leviticus and kept going), you probably found the books of Chronicles intensely annoying. Just when you seemed to getting somewhere in the story, Chronicles starts all over again from the beginning! Yes, that is exactly what Chronicles does, and aren't we fortunate, because it is a stunning exercise in reframing. Chronicles tells the story that Kings has just told, but in a new way. Much of Chronicles actually reproduces Kings verbatim. That makes it much easier for us to hone in on what is different and to work out what changes had to be made. Chronicles (and other books including Leviticus) help us to identify the new story and the new covenant theology that was developed after the return from exile.

If you have read *Abraham: A journey*, you may not be surprised to hear that I believe that Genesis was one of the other books most intimately connected with this post-exilic reframing. It operates like a prequel, which makes you look at everything that follows in a new light. Prequels are currently pretty big in the film world. They're popular with studios and audiences alike because they extend the life of a film franchise when the story seems otherwise to have nowhere else to go. By telling the *backstory,* you can change people's perceptions of the main story. Have you ever wanted to go back and rewatch a favourite film after you've seen its prequel? Did it seem different? Changing what happens at the *beginning* of a story can have a big impact on your understanding of what happens afterwards.

There were prequels in the biblical period too. Recent academic research has shown that adding new material at the beginning of an authoritative piece of writing was a common way of effecting revision in the Ancient Near East (among Israel's neighbours). Genesis, I believe, does just that. In *Abraham: A journey* I talked about the ways in which the story of Abraham recreates the experience of the returning exiles. He came to Canaan from Mesopotamia, via Haran in the north, and he arrived to find other people already in the land. He was given *new* promises by YHWH – of blessing, of children and of land. Because these were not the same as the promises that were broken by YHWH in the exile, they could be relied on, and much of Abraham's story (Genesis 15 is a good example) works hard to persuade its first audiences that God and God's promises could be trusted. I argued that Abraham's story is based on the story of David, but rewritten for a time when there is no king, so that the roles and responsibilities that had previously belonged to the monarch (like the administration of justice and righteousness) had to be exercised democratically by the people (see especially Gen. 18.17–19). Further, all of this had to take place in a nation where the gift of the land was not exclusive (i.e. there had been no expulsion of other peoples, as in Joshua and Judges), but in which God's chosen people had to learn to negotiate being neighbours with the various other groups of people also living in the land (as Abraham did, see especially Genesis 26).

Where does the story of Joseph fit into this? At the most basic level Joseph's story functions as a bridge between the story of Abraham and his descendants and the beginning of the story of the nation of Israel, in which the Israelites are being oppressed in slavery in Egypt. Joseph's story gets Jacob's family to Egypt, and it also introduces the idea of slavery, so that it is a surprise at the beginning of Exodus that the *Hebrews* are enslaved by the *Egyptians*. What else does Joseph's story do? I've argued here that it tells the 'which son will be chosen?' story for the sons of Jacob, which establishes the 12 tribes that become important later, and that sets up the tensions between the north and the south that come into play following the death of Solomon. I would also argue that it tells the story of a 'hero' of Israel who was, for better or worse, a pretty resilient fellow.

You and me and our stories

Joseph's story, and especially his lengthy imprisonment, encourages me to believe that there is time for me to work out what the next step in reframing my story might look like. It also encourages me not to lose hope as I continue to ride the roller-coaster of job applications and work out my vocation to preach the gospel in a new land. What do you see in Joseph's story that speaks to your life, or that suggests some reframing, whether minor or radical, that you think you might need to do for your story? Have you been thrust into new circumstances, whether by choice or not, that require you to 'cut your hair' and 'walk like an Egyptian' in order to move forward? What specific changes do you need to make in order to 'choose life'? If you have already made a change of that sort, how does it feel now to look back on it with the benefit of hindsight? Did you know at the time that you were re-inventing yourself, or are you just beginning to perceive that now? How do you now tell your story differently?

In this chapter we have been focusing mostly on our own (and Joseph's) ability to build resilience from within. In telling Joseph's story, I've honed in on how Joseph has presented and 'reframed' himself in the face of his trials. The second of the three resilience factors that I want to address is 'recruitability'. How good has Joseph been at accessing the resources that he needs to support him? We've already seen that Joseph is remarkably good at winning the confidence of strangers and co-opting them to 'Team Joseph'. How will he do when he comes face to face again with the brothers whose confidence he lost when he was just a boy and who went on to betray him? And how is Joseph doing with the confidence of God? He certainly had it during his enslavement and the early days of his imprisonment – has he lost that too? How genuine are his exclamations of piety? Are they part of his core or of one of his re-inventions of himself? The only way to find out is to read on.

4

The brothers

GENESIS 42—47.12

Now Joseph was governor over the land; it was he who sold to all the people of the land. And Joseph's brothers came and bowed themselves before him with their faces to the ground.[7] When Joseph saw his brothers, he recognized them, but he treated them like strangers and spoke harshly to them. (Gen. 42.6–7)

One of the really great things about being married to R. is that we're both writers. Even better, we both, in our different ways, write about stories. It is terrific to share such close interests – sometimes it's not easy to distinguish between work and play. As many similarities as we share, however, there is a very significant difference in our approach to writing. R. loves to get lots of people involved. Once he has a written draft, however rough, he wants to send it to lots of people to have them read it for him. He is absolutely fearless. He is fearless in the sense that he doesn't mind asking people to read very long pieces of his writing in relatively short periods of time. He is also fearless in the sense that he really welcomes their criticism. He works hard to polish his writing so that it reflects the observations that his readers have made, and the result is always that he comes up with a much improved final product –and he has been hugely successful as a writer as a result. (Okay, there are many other things about his writing that have contributed to his success!)

Now, I'm really quite different. I'm far more protective of my drafts. I want to keep them to myself until I am confident that they are ready to be seen in public. I am not fearless at all – I'm often really nervous about anyone else seeing my work (and I don't much like asking either). Why on earth I think that it will be any less frightening having someone read what I have written when it is already in print (and when it is therefore too late to fix) I have no idea, but that is just how it is with me. I take some comfort from the fact that quite a lot of writers are like me. Since I've come to London, for example, I've been lucky enough to get to know my very favourite author, who just happens to be a friend of R.'s (another of the really great things about being married to him!) She has always refused to allow anybody to see her drafts before they go to her publishers, and she's been *enormously* successful. But since knowing R., I've learned that it is a pretty good idea to let him, at least, read my work before I sign off on it. It is often a not-terribly-comfortable experience. I want to be told that my writing is wonderful, not that I need to go back and do lots more work on it! I don't take criticism especially well. Nevertheless, I've learned that a little bit of discomfort is definitely worth it. The rewrite is nearly always significantly better than my first attempt. It is still very much my writing, but R. has helped me to bring out its potential. And he has great ideas that I very often add in, and that sometimes wind up being other people's favourite bits.

The second resilience factor – 'recruiting'

I couldn't say that one of these two approaches to writing is 'better' than the other. One tends to come more naturally to some people, and the other more naturally to others. On the other hand, however, one of these approaches is almost certainly more *resilient* than the other. In the last chapter we considered the first of three resilience factors: 'reframing'. In this chapter we will turn to the second factor: 'recruiting'. (We'll also read an unusually long excerpt from the Joseph story – Chapter 42 of Genesis to halfway through Chapter 47.) Recruiting is all about the ability to attract the resources one needs to respond well to a stressful situation. 'Resources' may include just about anything, including people. R. is really good at recruiting people. At home he recruits me *constantly*! I tend to be less good at recruiting people – my tendency is to work alone. And I tend to like to guard my writing jealously as well. Yes, that is my style, and it fits generally with my introversion, but I am learning that getting the views of others before I press 'send' may not only be safer in terms of avoiding major gaffes, but is also likely to make my writing more readable.

There are other types of recruiting that I'm better at. Because of my experience of illness, I've got quite good at seeking professional help and advice. There have been a number of points in my life, for example, when I've recognized that I have needed to access some counselling or psychotherapy support to get me through a particularly challenging time. I'm also pretty good at calling plumbers and electricians at the slightest sign of trouble! Asking for help can feel like an expression of weakness, but in fact, it is a strength. We all need resources, and the willingness to seek them, together with an aptitude for attracting them (especially when they're people), is a major factor for resilience – arguably even the most important factor. This also means that having friends is enormously important for building resilience. Apparently six close, supportive friendships is considered to be ideal. I'm afraid I find that a bit of a challenging number. How about you?

Resilience, then, isn't just about putting our head down (or gritting our teeth) and getting on with it. It is also about acknowledging that we need help and being good at getting it. One of the extraordinary things that we are learning from research into how trauma manifests in the body is that, physiologically, we are built to be sociable animals. We need contact with others to function well. This is especially so when we are very, very young, but it is also true even when we're old and crusty. Social interaction stimulates our brains, slows our heart rate and makes us stronger. That is one of the reasons why the statistics that tell us that we are tending to be more solitary – living in solo accommodation or experiencing increasing isolation as we age – are so concerning. We learn and practice resilience best in company with others.

In Chapter Three, we concluded that Joseph's ability to 'reframe' his story and his identity pointed to his resilience. If we think back to consider Joseph's capacity for 'recruiting', we are likely to find that our impression of Joseph as resilient is confirmed on this head too, at least at first sight. We've seen that Joseph has displayed an extraordinary knack for recruiting others to his cause. Even betrayal, trafficking, enslavement and imprisonment don't get in the way of his making a positive impression on the authority figures he encounters. As a child, he becomes his father's openly acknowledged favourite. In Egypt he impresses and gains the confidence of Potiphar, then the chief jailer and finally Pharaoh, so that all three put him in charge of everything over which they have authority – first a household, then a jail and finally a kingdom.

There is, however, one group of people that Joseph signally fails to recruit to his cause. As a child he completely alienates each of his eleven brothers. To be fair, Jacob's unwise displays of parental favouritism are part of the problem, but even so, Joseph does a pretty good job of being unbearable all on his own. Crowing about his dreams of his brothers bowing down to him (Gen. 37.5–11) and accepting his father's assignments to spy on them (Gen. 37.14) were never calculated to win their affection. Joseph's brothers have been absent from the story (apart from the story about Judah – and Tamar – in Genesis 38) since Joseph's trafficking to Egypt, and so Joseph has not been faced with that particular legacy of his childhood. In Genesis 42, however, Joseph's brothers suddenly re-enter the story. How will he respond?

Joseph's brothers go to Egypt

Egypt is not the only place experiencing drought. There are drought conditions and shortages of food also in Canaan, and they impact upon Jacob and his family. So Jacob's brothers decide, along with many others, to go to Egypt to buy food. Jacob, however, doesn't send Benjamin on the Egyptian expedition because he fears 'that harm would come to him' (Gen. 42.4). What kind of harm is Jacob afraid of? Is it just that Benjamin is the youngest and the journey to Egypt might be dangerous, or is Jacob worried that Benjamin might suffer the same fate as Joseph? The text doesn't say, but arguably this is another instance of Jacob's favouritism.

Arriving in Egypt, the remaining brothers find themselves before Joseph, but they don't recognize their brother. They bow in front of him, thus unwittingly *almost* fulfilling one of Joseph's childhood dreams (Benjamin is missing). Joseph recognizes them immediately. He also remembers the dreams he'd had about them. Nevertheless, he treats them like strangers, speaking to them harshly and, even though they repeatedly assure him they have come from Canaan to buy food, he accuses them of being spies come to spy on the 'nakedness of the land'. Still concealing his true identity and swearing by the name of Pharaoh(!), he devises a test for the brothers. One of them must return to their father's house in Canaan and bring back their brother Benjamin while the others remain in prison. This is the only way they can prove to him that they are not spies. Joseph puts them all in prison for three days. After three days he returns and repeats the test, but with a slight modification – if they wish to live, *all* of the brothers should return to Canaan, carrying food for their households, leaving only one of their brothers behind. The brothers discuss this proposition in Joseph's presence, not realizing that he understands every word. Even though they don't recognize Joseph, they somehow understand their grim circumstances to be the penalty for their long-ago betrayal of Joseph. Reuben helpfully says, 'I told you so.' Joseph turns away briefly and weeps, before turning back and speaking to them once again. He chooses Simeon to remain behind and has him bound. Then he orders his servants to fill the brothers' bags with grain and add to the sack the money they had brought, as well as provisions for the journey.

Why does Joseph do all of this? Is he desperate to see Benjamin again? Alternatively, does he want *all* his brothers to bow down before him, thereby fulfilling his dream entirely? Or is he cold-heartedly playing with his brothers – demanding of them the one thing he knows would most pain his father? It is typical of Genesis to leave these kinds of questions about thoughts and motives hanging unanswered.

The brothers depart on their donkeys with their sacks. When they stop for the night, one opens his sack and sees the returned money. All of the brothers become very nervous, saying to one another, 'What is this that God has done to us?' (Gen. 42.28) When they arrive home, they tell Jacob the whole story; when they open their sacks to show him the food and they see that all of their money has been returned, they are all, father and sons, dismayed. For Jacob, the whole thing is about him: 'I am the one you have bereaved of children: Joseph is no more and Simeon is no more, and now you would take Benjamin. All this has happened to me!' Reuben tries to take the weight of the situation on himself by guaranteeing Benjamin's safety, telling Jacob that if he, Reuben, does not return with Benjamin, Jacob may kill Reuben's two sons. Jacob is not persuaded (after all, why should the deaths of two of his grandsons make the situation any better?), and his next words make it clear that he has learned no lessons about the dangers of parental favouritism: 'My son shall not go down with you, for his brother is dead, and he alone is left' (Gen. 42.38). Does Jacob really only care about Benjamin and Joseph, the two sons of his beloved Rachel?

So the brothers stay put in Canaan, eating their way through the food they'd brought back from Egypt. Eventually, when the food runs out and the famine has not yet eased, Jacob again asks his sons to go to Egypt to get food. Judah reminds Jacob about Joseph's demand that they not return without Benjamin. Jacob begins to complain again, but Judah steps in, offering to be surety for Benjamin: 'If I do not bring him back to you and set him before you, then let me bear the blame forever.' Eventually, Jacob relents and sends them on their way, with Benjamin, gifts for 'the man' and the returned money as well as new silver. When Joseph sees them bringing Benjamin, he instructs his steward to prepare a feast for him to eat with his brothers in his home. The brothers become nervous, worrying that Joseph is angry about the money they found in their sacks, but the steward reassures them that there is nothing to worry about.

When Joseph enters, the brothers offer him the gifts and again bow before him. This time, all eleven brothers, or 'stars', are present (Gen. 37.9). Joseph asks after their father, and they tell him that Jacob is alive and well. When Joseph sees Benjamin, he is overcome and has to go to an adjoining room for a short while to weep. When he returns, the meal is served. Joseph is served alone and the brothers by themselves and the other Egyptians by *them*selves, because for Egyptians, eating with a Hebrew was an abomination (Gen. 43.32). Joseph seats his brothers in exact order, from eldest to youngest, and the brothers are amazed. Joseph also sees that Benjamin receives five times as much food as his brothers, and they all eat and drink. Undisguised favouritism is alive and well in Jacob's family!

After the meal, Joseph instructs his steward to fill the brothers' sacks with food and to put their money on top of the food. Joseph also tells him to put Joseph's silver cup in Benjamin's sack. The brothers depart early the next morning, but shortly after they leave, Joseph asks his steward to follow them, catch them up and accuse them of stealing the cup. Joseph tells him that when he finds the cup, he should say to them, 'Why have you returned evil for good? Why have you stolen my silver cup? Is it not from this that my lord drinks? Does he not indeed use it for divination? You have done wrong in doing this.' (Gen. 44.4–5) The steward does it all as he has been asked. The brothers are shocked and protest their innocence, but when Joseph's steward opens their sacks one by one, he eventually finds the cup in Benjamin's sack (where, of course, he himself had placed it). The brothers tear their clothes, repack their sacks and turn around to return to the city.

When they come to Joseph's house, he is still there. They fall to the ground before him once again. Joseph asks them why they did it – do they not know that Joseph practises divination? Judah is the one who responds, 'What can we say to my lord? What can we speak? How can we clear ourselves? God has found out the guilt of your servants; here we are then, my lord's slaves, both we and also the one in whose possession the cup has been found.' (Gen. 44.16) But Joseph still has another card to play. He says, 'Far be it from me that I should do so! Only the one in whose possession the cup was found shall be my slave; but as for you, go up in peace to your father.' Joseph has no interest in detaining all his brothers – he just wants to keep Benjamin. The emotion and favouritism Joseph has displayed suggests that it is possible that he genuinely wants to be close to his only full brother (i.e. the son of both Rachel and Jacob). But Joseph's behaviour is so manipulative that it is also just possible that Joseph just wants to cause as much trouble between his brothers and his father as he can.

Joseph the recruiter?

What is Joseph playing at? What is his game? It seems difficult to find an interpretation that explains all of these baffling manoeuvres. At the beginning, it seems that Joseph is motivated by anger. Later, he seems to be affected by real emotion, especially for Benjamin. Nevertheless, his behaviour continues to be cruel. He certainly doesn't seem to have any undue regard for his father's happiness.

In this chapter, we have been focusing on the role of recruiting in building resilience. I've suggested that one of the essential factors of resilience is a capacity and aptitude for recruiting resources (including people) to one's cause. Viewed from some angles, Joseph displays both capacity and aptitude for recruiting his brothers. If his objectives are to see Benjamin, or to see his brothers bow and scrape before him, or to punish his brothers – or a combination of all three – then he seems to be achieving these goals fairly effectively. He is doing a great job of moving the pieces around his particular chosen chessboard. Of course, he is not in the process doing anything to repair his relationship with his brothers. And for all the apparent affection he has for Benjamin, we are given no indication about Benjamin's feelings for Joseph.

All of this throws up rather a difficult question. If behaviour that could be described as 'manipulative' is effective for achieving one's chosen ends, can it also be described as 'resilient'? And if not, why not? Does being resilient necessarily entail maintaining good relationships with people, or treating them well? And does it necessarily entail having an overall objective or aspiration that is 'healthy'? We will return to these questions.

There is a possibility that I've not fully canvassed yet in relation to Joseph's treatment of his brothers. Perhaps Joseph has no clearly defined sense of what he wants from his renewed acquaintance with them. Perhaps, too, Joseph is carrying unresolved trauma from his brothers' betrayal of him and his subsequent enslavement and imprisonment. If these suggestions are on the money, then Joseph may not have any clear, *conscious* sense of what he's doing with his brothers at all. He will be being driven by an unconscious need to reconstruct the events of the original trauma, with himself playing either the role of victim or of perpetrator.

You will remember that we have already talked about the 'compulsion to repeat' that is often felt by trauma victims. I even suggested that in Joseph's rejection of Mrs Potiphar's advances, there was a hint of repetition of Joseph's betrayal, in that once again he found himself naked and incarcerated, with his robe being used as false evidence about him. What about Joseph's treatment of his brothers – is there any hint of repetition here? Actually, there is – and more than just a hint. Joseph's Egyptian fate was to be enslaved and then imprisoned. Joseph himself does it the other way around – imprisoning his brothers and then discussing their enslavement to him. He throws his brothers in prison for three days before allowing them to return to Canaan (Gen. 42.16–17), apart from Simeon, whom he has bound as a slave (Gen. 42.24). On the brothers' second visit, after their abortive departure and the discovery of the silver cup, Judah offers the brothers to Joseph as slaves. Joseph responds by saying that only Benjamin will be his slave. There might even be a hint of repetition in Joseph's replacement of the brothers' money in their sacks (Gen. 42.25; 44.2). Is there a sense here in which Joseph is 'buying' his brothers, just as they 'sold' him?

If we can look at Joseph's behaviour as part of a trauma reaction, then we can dodge, for the moment, that extremely difficult question about whether behaviour can be both manipulative and resilient. If Joseph really is acting without a *conscious* sense of his objectives, but is being motivated by an unconscious drive to reconstruct the trauma, then his behaviour cannot be characterized as resilient. This is not a 'bouncing back' from a stressful experience, but an impulsive reaction to it. Joseph is not the master of his impulses and actions, but rather the helpless victim of them.

You and Joseph

How are you feeling about Joseph at the moment, as a character? You'll remember that I said in the first chapter that Joseph has typically been held in high regard by both Jews and Christians. He is often seen, in particular, as a model of wisdom. He is held up as a saviour both of Israel and Egypt. Through his foresight and planning, there was enough food to sustain his large family (and other Canaanites) through a seven-year famine, as well as the entire nation of Egypt. And his capacity to win the confidence of people – Jacob, Potiphar, his jailer and finally Pharaoh – was enormous. You may have begun reading this book with a view of Joseph along those lines (and, certainly, Joseph is portrayed as a hero in the stage show). If so, it is quite possible that your view of Joseph has been shaken a little by these first chapters. In particular, you might not previously have thought through the implications of his treatment of his brothers. Perhaps you are now feeling angry toward him, or at least disapproving of some of his behaviour. However, it might also be the case that one of the emotions you are feeling about Joseph is pity. You may feel moved for him that he has experienced such difficult things, and you may have compassion for his impulsive behaviour under all the circumstances.

Do you know or live with somebody who is struggling with unresolved trauma? Perhaps they have actually been diagnosed with Post-Traumatic Stress Disorder (PTSD) or Obsessive-Compulsive Disorder (OCD) or any one of a number of related conditions. If so, you will have experience of the internal struggle between being angry with, frustrated at or disapproving of them, on the one hand, and having compassion for them on the other, even in the wake of dreadful behaviour that hurts yourself or others. You may deal daily with the struggle of loving somebody who is in the grip of trauma response, knowing that they are to some degree incapable of fully regulating their own words and actions, while at the same time knowing the hurt that is being done both to them and to you, and wanting to stop it.

Perhaps the trauma victim is yourself. Maybe you observe some of your own behaviour with a sense of helplessness, feeling compassion for the people you hurt, while at the same time hoping that the people around you will see past your behaviour to the real wounded you, buried inside. Perhaps you don't know why you act in certain ways, why you seem to bring disaster upon yourself repeatedly or why you can't seem to prevent yourself from hurting others.

If either of those two scenarios rings bells for you, how do you feel about that, and how does that impact on how you relate to Joseph and his story?

Since beginning the work on trauma that I'm currently engaged in, I've had the interesting and challenging experience of thinking about my own experience of trauma. Recent research has suggested that trauma response may be the cause, or part of the cause, of ME. The proposal makes some intuitive sense in that both trauma and ME involve irregularities of the central nervous system. Further, adrenalin (and recovery from adrenalin-flooding) seems to play a significant role in both. I've had to consider my own behaviour and the ways in which I tend to react to certain stimuli. I don't recall having experienced a major trauma, and I'm not aware of having flashbacks, or periods of time when I've dissociated myself from my body. But these things do not necessarily mean that I *or one of my ancestors* (!) didn't experience a major trauma that is still affecting my health today (the field of epigenetics is generating disconcerting findings that trauma can be handed down from one generation to the next, so that the physiology of a child can be impacted by trauma experienced by the parent). Part of my experience of ME has been learning to have compassion for myself. Having compassion for others, even when they behave in ways I don't particularly approve of, is one of the lessons I'm still learning.

Trauma and biblical narrative

Before we get back to Joseph's story, this might be a good time to say something more about trauma and reading the Bible. I've been making a number of suggestions about Joseph and his motivations for acting in certain ways. In my discussion I've been treating Joseph as an historical person and making suppositions about the impact that the events of his life, as described in the pages of Genesis, may have had upon him and his behaviour. In doing this, I don't mean to be suggesting definitely that there was a person called Joseph some three thousand years ago and that he was a trauma victim. I certainly don't mean to be suggesting that the author(s) of the Joseph story set about writing an account of a traumatized person. Joseph may actually have existed – or his story, which may have reflected some aspects of real historical memory, may have been told in Israel for many generations before being written down. It is impossible to be certain about Joseph's historicity from this distance, without extra-biblical evidence to support it.

What I have been doing is using trauma as a 'lens' for interpreting the Joseph story. If I wanted to be posh or technical, I'd say 'heuristic lens', but all I really mean is something like a pair of glasses that can help one to see something familiar in a different way, or the way that a good lens in a camera or telescope can suddenly bring blurred things into a new focus. I have been asking what new aspects or meaning can be drawn out of the Joseph story when you read it through the lens of what we know today about the impact of trauma. I have also been using Joseph's story as a vehicle for exploring resilience and how resilience might or might not work in our lives today, regardless of whether there is any historical basis for Joseph and his behaviour and that of his family.

There is one other respect, however, in which scholars of the Bible think about the Bible and trauma. As I've already said, scholars are becoming more aware that the Old Testament writers themselves experienced major traumas, especially in the events of the destruction of Jerusalem and the experience of exile. These same scholars are engaged in exploring how those experiences of trauma impacted their writing. For example, can we see in biblical text evidence of the symptoms of unresolved trauma? Such evidence might include the telling of inherently violent stories or storytelling that is incoherent because of details that are missing or disordered, in the same way that the stories of trauma victims today tend to be patchy or disordered. This kind of reading can involve more than just using trauma as an interpretive lens, that is, how does thinking about trauma help me to read this passage differently? It can involve educated guesses about the factors that influenced the way in which the biblical text was written. For example, an argument is sometimes made that the Gospels (perhaps with the exception of Mark, which is generally considered to have been written prior to the destruction of Jerusalem in 70 AD) reflect the trauma experienced by the evangelists during and after that very dramatic event. So, while I'd be very uncomfortable about suggesting that the authors of Genesis deliberately wrote the Joseph story about an actual traumatized person, I'm much more comfortable with the idea that in telling the Joseph story, the authors were influenced by their own experiences of trauma or by behaviours they'd observed in others or in themselves.

Judah steps up

We need to get back to the story. And we're coming back to a special moment – the moment when Judah comes into his own and takes on the mantle of leader of the brothers. Judah makes a speech. It is one of the longest speeches in Genesis (just topping the servant's speech in Genesis 24 but falling short of Jacob's blessing in Genesis 49). Judah tells the story of the brothers' journeys to Egypt and describes the sorrow Jacob will feel if they return without Benjamin. He says that he has given an undertaking to Jacob to be surety for Benjamin and asks Joseph to have compassion and allow him (Judah) to remain as Joseph's slave and Benjamin to return with his brothers.

Judah's speech melts something in Joseph. Joseph becomes emotional again, but this time, instead of going off to weep in private, he sends all of his servants out and he finally reveals his identity to his brothers. Then he weeps so loudly that even Pharaoh's household hears him. He asks again after Jacob, but his brothers are dismayed and cannot answer. Joseph tells them not to be distressed about their treatment of him. It was God's will that Joseph should be in Egypt in order to 'preserve life': 'God sent me before you to preserve for you a remnant on earth, and to keep alive for you many survivors. So it was not you who sent me here, but God; he has made me a father to Pharaoh, and lord of all his house and ruler over all the land of Egypt.' (Gen. 45.7–8) Joseph tells his brothers that they must tell Jacob how much he, Joseph, is honoured in Egypt and about everything they have seen. Then he and Benjamin fall on each other's necks and weep, after which Joseph kisses his other brothers and talks with them.

When Pharaoh and his servants learn that Joseph has been reunited with his brothers, they are pleased. Pharaoh says to Joseph:

> Say to your brothers, 'Do this: load your animals and go back to the land of Canaan. Take your father and your households and come to me, so that I may give you the best of the land of Egypt, and you may enjoy the fat of the land.' You are further charged to say, 'Do this: take wagons from the land of Egypt for your little ones and for your wives, and bring your father, and come. Give no thought to your possessions, for the best of all the land of Egypt is yours.' (Gen. 45.17–20)

All of this Joseph says to his brothers, and they do as Pharaoh has directed. Joseph gives his brothers wagons and provisions for the journey and a set of garments each. To Benjamin, he gives 300 pieces of silver and five sets of garments. He also sends gifts for Jacob. As they are departing, he can't resist saying to his brothers, 'Do not quarrel along the way.'

When they arrive back in Canaan, they tell Jacob that Joseph is still alive and that he is ruler over the land of Egypt (Gen. 45.26). Jacob is stunned. At first he doesn't believe them, but after they tell him the whole story and show him Joseph's gifts, he revives, saying, 'Enough! My son Joseph is still alive. I must go and see him before I die.' And with that, Jacob and the rest of his family set out for Egypt.

At this point, the story gets all religious for a bit. The caravan travels as far as Beer-sheba, where Jacob stops to sacrifice to the God of his father, Isaac. God calls to Jacob, saying, 'Jacob, Jacob!' Jacob says, 'Here I am,' and God speaks to him. God tells Jacob that he shouldn't be afraid to go to Egypt and makes him three promises: to make him a great nation, to bring him back from Egypt to Canaan and that his son Joseph will bury him at his death. After that conversation, the caravan sets out again for Egypt, although, oddly, it reads as though they are setting out for the first time, because the narrator describes the travellers and their vehicles at *great* length. At some point, it seems, a scribe has added a 'religious bit' to what would otherwise have been a straightforward travelogue and list of travellers. Why might he have done that? In fact, there are a number of these added 'religious bits' throughout Genesis. If you have read *Abraham: A journey,* you will have encountered several. You might even find that your memory is being jogged, because they tend to contain a number of similar elements. So, for example, in verses 1 and 11 of Genesis 22 (the story of God's near-sacrifice of Isaac), God had called, 'Abraham, Abraham' and Abraham replied, 'Here I am!' The promise to make Jacob 'a great nation' you might also recall from the Abraham story. The same promise is made to Abraham, Ishmael (twice, but never Isaac, curiously) and now Jacob. A final common feature is that in a number of these 'religious bits', God gives travel instructions. So, whereas God here tells Jacob not to be afraid to go to Egypt, in Gen 26.2 God tells Isaac *not* to go to Egypt, but to remain in Gerar. The real point or function of all these inserted passages seems to be to build a kind of framework for Genesis, binding the stories of each of the ancestors and their families together. The shape of the story is maintained, and God's faithfulness is demonstrated when the same conversations and the same divine promises occur in succeeding generations.

We are almost at the end of the story for this chapter! When they are nearing their destination, Jacob sends Judah on ahead to meet

Joseph. When he sees that the travellers are approaching, Joseph leaps into his chariot and rides up to meet his father. He falls on his father's neck and weeps for a good while. Jacob says, 'I can die now, having seen for myself that you are still alive.' Joseph then rides back to alert Pharaoh to his family's arrival, after carefully tutoring his family in what to say to Pharaoh when they are presented to him. Pharaoh directs Joseph to allow his family to settle in the best part of the land, in a place called Goshen, and to choose the most reliable of his brothers to have the care of Pharaoh's own livestock. Pharaoh also meets Jacob and asks his age after which Jacob blesses Pharaoh. The story of Joseph's family settling in Egypt ends with a description of Joseph finding a place for them to settle, as Pharaoh had directed, in the best part of the land, and providing them with food.

There is one final, strange detail to mention before we leave the story for now. It is a detail that seems to point toward the forward movement of the story and that is also curiously pertinent, given our focus (or 'lens') on trauma and resilience. Even though I mentioned the place 'Goshen' only once in the last paragraph, it is mentioned several times in the biblical text – in fact six times in two paragraphs. It appears that Goshen is not only good land, but also ideal for pasturing the herds and flocks that Jacob's family has brought with them. Therefore it is remarkable that the description of Joseph's carrying out of Pharaoh's generous instructions concerning Joseph's family reads as follows: 'Joseph settled his father and his brothers, and granted them a holding in the land of Egypt, in the best part of the land, in the land of *Rameses*, as Pharaoh had instructed.' (Gen. 47.11) Where has 'Rameses' come from all of a sudden? It is impossible to know for certain whether this sudden reference to Rameses is simply an error, or represents an alternative tradition, or is designed to deliver a deliberate surprise or shock to the reader. It is the first time in Genesis that Rameses has been mentioned. But it is probably a name that is familiar to you. Do you recognize it? Rameses is one of the two supply cities (along with Pithom) in which the Israelites are enslaved at the beginning of Exodus (Exodus 1:11). Here is both a connection between the Joseph and Moses stories *and* a slightly chilling forewarning about how all of this is going to turn out for the children of Jacob.

Joseph the recruiter? (again)

We have been reading Joseph's story in the light of different resilience 'factors'. In Chapter Three we considered 'reframing', and I pointed to the ways in which Joseph had successfully 'reframed' or 're-invented' himself as an Egyptian, thereby earning Pharaoh's complete trust. In this chapter I have referred in passing to two more 'Egyptianizing' behaviours that Joseph adopts. Did you notice them? At one point Joseph swears 'by the name of Pharaoh'. At another, Joseph tells his brothers (and even instructs his servant to tell his brothers) that he practises divination. These are very Egyptian things to do, but they also raise questions about the nature of Joseph's continuing relationship with God. It is clear from Josh 23.7 that an Israelite ought not to swear by the name of the god of one of the surrounding nations (and remember, Pharaoh is revered as both divine and royal), but only by the God of Israel (e.g. Ps. 63.11), while divination is prohibited in Deuteronomy 18.10, along with child sacrifice, soothsaying, augury and sorcery. (At the time of Joseph, of course, in the world of the story, the laws of Deuteronomy had not yet been given, but the author(s) of the Joseph story would certainly have known them. We probably ought to assume that by associating Joseph clearly with a forbidden behaviour of that type, the author of that particular passage wanted to send his readers a coded, and probably negative, message about Joseph.)

In this chapter, we have moved on to consider 'recruiting' and, particularly, recruiting of people. The picture we've drawn of Joseph in that regard is a curious one. Up until now, the Joseph we've got to know has exhibited an extraordinary talent for charming and winning the trust of authority figures that he's encountered. His early relationship with his brothers, however, proved him to be clueless when dealing with his equals. Every aspect of his self-focused behaviour seemed calculated to earn their mistrust and hatred. Once the brothers had taken their ultimate revenge, selling Joseph into slavery, Joseph no longer had to deal with the consequences of that behaviour – until, that is, the brothers arrived in Egypt. At that point Joseph's behaviour becomes confusing. He is clearly emotionally affected by being reunited with his brothers, but the narrator says little about his state of mind, and his actions tell us only a little more. If Joseph's goal, upon the arrival of his brothers, is to be reunited with his father and his only full brother, Benjamin, then you'd have to acknowledge that he achieves that. He achieves it by rather Machiavellian methods, but he achieves it, moving his brothers around like recalcitrant pieces on a chess board, with little or no care about the impact on them or on his father. Does this all go to further support the case for Joseph as resilient?

Or is something else going on? Is Joseph rather flailing around, unsure of his deepest desires, and the puppet of his own trauma injury – returning his injury eye for eye, tooth for tooth, albeit subconsciously? If that is the case, then his actions are not the actions of a resilient person at all. They are the actions of a person who is hurting and who cannot perceive and respond to his own wound.

There is a further way of 'reading' Joseph's actions – one that holds the other two together, in tension. You might recall that earlier, when I was talking about the compulsion to repeat, I said that the subconscious driver of the compulsion is a desire to recreate the circumstances of the initial trauma in the hope that *this time* there might be a healing response. What the traumatized person subconsciously craves is an opportunity to relive the experience in which they do and feel everything necessary for the body and brain to fully work through and release the trauma response. Mostly, unfortunately, these repetitions of the original trauma end disastrously for everybody, more often than not creating new trauma responses in innocent bystanders.

Have you ever watched a dog shaking after escaping a dangerous situation? Animals know instinctively how to react to being overwhelmed. They work the shock and the emotions out through physical movement – including shaking. People do this too, of course, although rather less dramatically. Trauma writer Peter Levine writes about the very physical way that animals process trauma, including animals like tigers that need to engage in dangerous encounters in order to get food. He observes that this physical expression of trauma that animals seem to know by instinct is highly effective at processing trauma and working it out of the system, so that it is not stored in the body for the long term. If an animal is stuck, however, under a tree or the body of another animal, for example, it will not be physically able to process the trauma – to get it out. The same thing happens to people. Those who are able to take some form of physical action in response to a trauma (even making someone a cup of tea!) or to express emotion in some physical form are more likely to get through an experience of being overwhelmed without developing a long-term trauma response. When people 'recreate' the scene of a trauma, they are subconsciously attempting to heal their trauma response by giving themselves another chance to 'shake' the trauma out of their bodies. They will go on to do this until either they are successful or the trauma is healed by some other means.

One way of reading what happens between Joseph and his brothers is to see it as a re-enactment *that succeeds*. Joseph's bizarre manipulation of his brothers on this occasion leads to Judah's eloquent speech that so moves something in Joseph that he is at last able to take action to resolve the trauma. Unable physically to control himself, he sends his attendants away and reveals himself to his brothers, kissing them and weeping on their necks. It might just be that Joseph has finally managed to process the trauma of his betrayal at the hands of his brothers, through the agency of Judah and his speech. There is a smallish sign in the story that supports this reading. When, later in Chapter 45, Joseph provisions his brothers for their return journey to Canaan, he gives each one of them a garment. This is a lovely inversion of the brothers' earlier action of stripping Joseph of his robe. Perhaps some genuine healing and reconciliation has taken place.

Resilience, recruiting and manipulation

Whichever way you look at it, Joseph's behaviour is bizarre. Perhaps the real question is whether it is conscious (and therefore manipulative) or subconscious (and therefore an expression of trauma response, even if it does turn out to be a successful healing strategy). The most difficult question arises if Joseph is conscious of his actions. Put baldly, is recruiting still resilient if it is manipulative?

Instinctively, we want to deny that manipulation of others can be resilient behaviour. That conclusion doesn't fit well with our society's current love affair with resilience, and it seems to be saying that something of which we disapprove can be of value.

It has taken me quite some time to come around to it, but I have to conclude that manipulative recruiting can be resilient behaviour. Manipulation can be a very effective (if not empathetic or caring) tool for persuading others to act in ways that benefit us. There is one qualification, however, that I need to make to my conclusion, and that is that it may be instructive to consider the long-term as well as short-term effects of manipulation. Looked at from a short-term viewpoint, it is very difficult to avoid the conclusion that manipulative behaviour can be resilient, perhaps spectacularly so. Considered from the perspective of the mid- or long-term, however, the picture may look different. What might start out as a highly effective, albeit manipulative, strategy might backfire over time, as those recruited cotton on to the manipulation being exerted over them and then simply refuse to co-operate at all. In the long term, then, our gut feelings about manipulation and resilience might turn out to be quite right, but I think we shouldn't rule out the possibility that something of which we disapprove may be labelled resilient, at least in the short-term.

I *feel* slightly more comfortable about my conclusion once that qualification has been added. It just suits my sense of right and wrong better. How about yours? I am afraid to say that the questions will not get any easier once we come to consider the third resilience factor, 'resolve', in the next chapter. Once again, we will be confronted with questions that bring us face to face with the less edifying aspects of resilience. We will also learn the outcome of Joseph's master plan to 'save' Egypt. Will he be Egypt's saviour, and if so, at what cost?

5

The saviour

They said, 'You have saved our lives; may it please my lord, we
will be slaves to Pharaoh'. (Gen. 47.25)

One of the biggest recent TV successes has been a serialization of
Margaret Atwood's classic novel from the 1980s, *The Handmaid's
Tale*. Atwood's dystopian novel presents a future in which toxic pol-
lution (among other factors) has significantly diminished human
fertility, so that society is organized around childbirth – fertile
women are put at the disposal of upper-class infertile couples, while
'criminals' such as homosexuals are publicly executed and their bodies hung on city walls as a warning to others. One of the striking
things about the novel is that this radically religious society takes
Genesis as a kind of constitution. The blessing, or imperative, found
in Genesis 1.28 and elsewhere, 'Be fruitful and multiply!' becomes
its central charter.

One of the centrepieces of life in this future 'Gilead' is the
monthly 'ceremony', in which a fertile 'handmaid' lies between the
legs of her mistress while being penetrated by her mistress' husband,
in the presence of the entire household. A fortunate handmaid will
eventually fall pregnant as a result and bear a 'viable' baby. The baby
will become the child of her mistress and master, and she will be
released from service. An unfortunate handmaid, however, who
has not produced a child after periods of 'service' in three households, with three masters, will be executed or sent to the colonies to
work with toxic waste (in reality, just a more gradual form of death

sentence). At the commencement of each monthly ceremony, the master reads aloud from the story of Jacob, in which Jacob produces children with his wives' maids, Bilhah and Zilpah, as well as with Leah and Rachel themselves. This story is used as the model for Gilead's enforced surrogacy regime. (Interestingly, Atwood cites the Jacob story exclusively, even though Abram and Sarai's use of Sarai's maid Hagar as surrogate in Genesis 16 is in some ways a more graphic illustration.)

Atwood's dystopian society is faced with a major public crisis: without sufficient levels of fertility, a society has no long-term prospect of survival. Today, we would almost certainly respond to a crisis of this sort with technology such as in-vitro fertilization, but Atwood has said that she wanted to limit her novel to technology that was readily available in the 1980s. Her futuristic Gilead responds instead with a radical puritanism that recognizes God as the source of life and that seeks to harness this gift by the enforced observance of strict 'holiness', in which enslavement and abasement of some residents (enforced by horrific punishments) is tolerated for the sake of the future of the society as a whole.

If you have seen the television series, but not read Atwood's book, you will not know that the novel reveals that Gilead is eventually dismantled and replaced by a more recognizable Western society. Atwood doesn't tell the reader how long Gilead lasted, but there are factors that suggest that it may have lasted quite a long time before eventually coming to an end. Nor does Atwood offer any assessment of whether or not Gilead was a resilient society ('resilience' wasn't quite the buzzword in the 1980s that it is now). Given everything you've read so far, do you have an opinion? If you know the story, you will almost certainly consider Gileadean society to be unacceptably oppressive. But does that necessarily mean that it can't also be resilient? Surely, desperate times may require, and justify, desperate measures? Perhaps, in a crisis, desperate measures can be considered resilient? But if a society can be both oppressive and resilient at the same time, even if in a context of crisis, does that affect how you feel about resilience?

'Resolve'

The third of the three resilience factors I'm addressing here is 'resolve'. It is the most difficult of the three to come to terms with – for me, anyway. I recently had a sobering experience. I was telling my spiritual director about this book and about finding resolve the most difficult of the three factors. He looked me in the eye and said, 'I'm not at all surprised that you find resolve difficult.' At first I didn't know what he meant, but it came to me fairly quickly. The whole time I have been meeting with him I have been struggling with my resolve. When I met R., my daily routine and my spiritual disciplines went out the window. I've always loved routine, and I found daily disciplines relatively easy as a single person. As part of a couple, living in a new country, I've discovered that it has been much harder to keep up my old disciplines; in fact I've been completely hopeless at it. This struggle has been one of the defining features of my life in the United Kingdom. So with this warning – that my account of resolve may have been influenced by this struggle – let's look more closely at resolve.

What does resolve mean in this context? Most of what we've been considering until now has been concerned with flexibility. This was especially true of the first factor, 'reframing'. Resolve sounds, at first blush, rather like the opposite. It seems to envisage that one determines on a certain course of action and then sticks to it, whatever the pressures to do otherwise. If Atwood's fictional Gilead can be assessed as resilient, then surely it is resilient in this way. If there is one thing that marks out Gilead society, it is rigidity. Everybody accepts that life is hierarchical, and they (mostly) stick to it for the sake of survival. To be fair, life in Gilead doesn't seem to be much fun for anybody. (Apart, perhaps, for Aunt Lydia, who seems to respond to the new regime with a depressing glee.) Even for the high-class men, who are able to escape the daily tedium from time to time, life seems to be essentially lonely and empty.

A couple of writers have been especially helpful for me around thinking about resolve, and especially around its apparent difference from flexibility. The first is a Dutch academic who writes in the area of narrative theology, R. Ruard Ganzevoort. Ganzevoort suggests that there are three essential models of resilience, each resilient in its own way. The first is perhaps the one we'd think of first: a flexible tree standing for years and years in a strong wind, perhaps gnarled and bent, but growing and thriving in a hostile environment. The second is one you might not have thought of: a sand dune. Sand dunes move and change their shape over time, especially when they are, like trees, subjected to wind. Over a very long period of time, a sand dune might lose every single one of its original grains of sand – all having been blown away – and yet the sand dune, as a whole, remains. This is a very radical kind of flexibility – infinite malleability. To some extent, the human body is like this – constantly shedding bits of itself, but always remaining essentially the same body. The third of Ganzevoort's models is that of resistance, represented by a rock. This is the one that perhaps most resembles Atwood's dystopia, and our 'resolve'. A rock will not be moved, except by the strongest wind, or perhaps by the constant attrition of waves. The extraordinary formations along the Great Ocean Road in southern Australia are a graphic example of how the sea can shape rock faces and outcrops over thousands of years. When you go to see them, you don't really know whether to marvel most at the extraordinary shapes of the standing rocks or at the very fact that they are still standing.

Ganzevoort's three models are very different, and yet each, in its own way, demonstrates resilience. These different approaches help me to see how very different kinds of behaviour can be considered resilient.

The other writer is Viktor L. Frankl, who wrote about his experiences as an inmate of Auschwitz. He addressed the crucially important question – what kind of mindset was needed in order to survive the horrors of the concentration camp? Three initial things strike me about his responses to the question. The first is that one had to be prepared to do *whatever it took* to survive, no matter how that might impact on other people. Survival depended upon total single-mindedness. There was no room for ethical niceties. The second thing that strikes me is his proposition that hope can be *dangerous*. Certainly, some foundational level of hopefulness in one's mindset was necessary in the camp, but setting one's hope on particular times or events was often lethal. Frankl wrote about inmates who focused their hopes on being home by Christmas. For a while, this hope was motivating, but as Christmas approached and it became less and less likely that the deadline would be achieved, resolve began to crumble. For the most part, those who had nursed this particular hope, and who had been motivated by it for months and months of hellish existence, were found dead in their beds sometime between Christmas and New Year.

The third part of Frankl's work that really strikes me is his conviction that theological argument and debate was a luxury that the inmates of concentration camps could not afford. This was not an appropriate context in which to ask oneself whether there was a God, or what one could properly expect of God in terms of God's salvific activity. One could not ask, 'what do I require of God?' There was only one appropriate question that one could ask oneself in such circumstances: 'what does God require of me in this situation?' Once one had the answer to that question, which might be simply 'survive!' or might involve advocacy or care for another, etc., one should simply go about doing it and ask no more questions. Not only was this the only question, it was a question essential to survival. One could survive only if one believed that one's survival was a duty owed to a force outside oneself. I can think of situations in which survivors of terrible ordeals have said that they owed their survival to a conviction that they must survive for the sake of their children, spouse, dog, etc. For Christians, however, I think that this has a great deal to say about the power and importance of living one's life in accordance with a sense of vocation to whatever life it is to which God is calling one.

I will come back to Frankl's ideas, in particular, as we move through the chapter and as we read further through Joseph's story. How do these reflections and resolve and the example of 'The Handmaid's Tale' relate to Joseph's next experience?

In our bit of the story for this chapter, Joseph finds himself facing a crisis that, while not exactly the same as the crisis facing Gilead in Atwood's novel, is just as serious. Do you remember back to Chapter Three? Joseph was finally able to leave his jail cell when he impressed Pharaoh with his interpretation of Pharaoh's dreams. Joseph told Pharaoh that the dreams meant that seven good years in Egypt would be followed by seven years of famine. He recommended to Pharaoh that Pharaoh hire somebody to collect and store grain during the good years, so that Egypt and the surrounding nations would survive the bad years. Pharaoh promptly hired Joseph. He made Joseph second only to himself in importance in Egypt. In Chapter Four we read about the ways in which Joseph put these plans into action, so that Egypt became the only nation in its region with reserves of food when the famine took hold. Even Joseph's own family came to Egypt to buy food and, eventually, were reunited with their lost son and brother.

Joseph, surely, was the hero of the day – the saviour of both Egypt and its neighbours! But at the very end of Chapter Three, we saw a hint that there might be another side to the story. Even though Joseph had compelled the Egyptian people to give Pharaoh their produce during the seven good years, once the bad years arrived, Joseph would not *give*, but *sell*, the gathered food back to the very Egyptians who had grown it and from whom it had been compulsorily acquired. Often, interpretations of the Joseph story gloss over this point, and you may be forgiven if you have not noticed it before in your own reading. We will consider Joseph's actions carefully, however, and it is possible that by the end of this chapter you will find yourself taking the view that Joseph's methods are every bit as oppressive as those of Atwood's Gilead. Yes, Joseph saves Egypt and its neighbours, but do the ends justify the means? And what does any of this have to do with resilience and, in particular, with resolve?

Joseph in crisis

The famine begins to take hold, and the Egyptians run out of food. They come to Joseph to ask for some of the grain that he had collected from them during the good years. Not only does Joseph *sell* them the grain rather than *give* it, he sells it at a premium – demanding all of the money that the people have. The people have no choice but to pay up, and Joseph takes all of the collected silver to Pharaoh's palace.

Inevitably, the food that the people have bought runs out. So they come back to Joseph, confessing that they have no more money and asking him to give them food anyway. 'Why should we starve in front of your eyes?' they ask. Joseph doesn't respond quite as the Egyptians expect. He tells them to bring him their livestock – flocks and herds and goats – and he will give them food in exchange for their animals. Over the course of a year, Joseph takes from the people all of their livestock in exchange for grain. Now the people have neither money to buy grain nor animals to provide them with milk or meat.

At the end of the year, the people have nothing left and again they approach Joseph to beg for food:

> We cannot hide from my lord that our money is all spent; and the herds of cattle are my lord's. There is nothing left in the sight of my lord but our bodies and our lands. Shall we die before your eyes, both we and our land? Buy us and our land

in exchange for food. We with our land will become slaves to Pharaoh; just give us seed, so that we may live and not die, and that the land may not become desolate. (Gen. 47.18b–19)

This time Joseph does precisely what the Egyptians ask – he buys their land and buys the people themselves as slaves for Pharaoh. 'He made slaves of them from one end of Egypt to the other.' (Gen. 47.21) Only one group of people is not required to sell their land to Joseph – the priests. The text explains that the priests receive an allowance from Pharaoh, on which they live. The text does not, however, remind the reader that Joseph's Egyptian wife is the daughter of a priest, so that his new family is spared from the loss of land and enslavement that is the lot of other Egyptians.

In exchange for the people's land and liberty, Joseph gives them seed and tells them to plant it. He instructs them that when it comes time for harvest, they are to keep four fifths themselves, but give one fifth to Pharaoh, and that they should continue to do so not only for the duration of the famine but in perpetuity. 'So Joseph made it a statute concerning the land of Egypt, and it stands to this day, that Pharaoh should have the fifth.' (Gen. 47.26a) In this way, Joseph gives the emergency measures a life that outlasts the emergency. In fact, it was not unusual in ancient Egypt and its neighbour nations that ordinary people should pay a tithe to the monarch (see, for example, Gen. 14.20). However, this tithe was typically paid from the spoils of war, and it was only ten per cent and not 20 per cent, as here. Joseph achieves here something new for Pharaoh.

Have you noticed Joseph developing a bit of an appetite for enslaving people? First it was his brothers, and now it is the Egyptian people. The fact that foreigners, including his own family, are coming to him to buy food suggests that Joseph's plan for the seven good years and the seven bad has been uniquely successful. But did he have to impoverish, and then enslave, the people of Egypt in order to achieve that success? It is difficult to resist the impression that Joseph has reverted to his childhood behaviour – betraying his peers (his brothers/the Egyptian people) in order to curry favour with his superior (Jacob/Pharaoh). One can only assume that Pharaoh looked kindly on Joseph's opportunism – appreciating the fact that his new right-hand man had not only got the country through famine, but had managed to fill Pharaoh's coffers in the process.

The lure of power

You might have thought that having gone through everything that he had, Joseph would be slow to mistreat other people. He knows exactly what it feels like to be betrayed, oppressed and eventually enslaved. How is it that he can go on to treat others in exactly the same way? I wonder whether you have ever behaved a little bit like Joseph in this regard – first railing at an injustice that has been done to you, and then, as soon as you have some power, doing precisely the same injustice to somebody else? I had an experience of this while I was at university that really surprised me, and I've never forgotten it.

While I was an undergraduate, I lived in a university college – St George's College in Perth, Western Australia. St George's was built to look like an Oxbridge college and as students we did our best to cultivate obscure and eccentric 'traditions' that we thought felt a bit 'Oxbridge'. The college had a half-wooded dining hall with a high table and lots of portraits of long-dead dons around the walls. At meals, undergraduates would sit at three long tables with benches that ran the entire length of the hall. The tradition was that first-year students, known as 'freshers', were not permitted to sit at the middle table – they could only sit at one or other of the outer tables. The inevitable result of this tradition was that the more senior students saw it as their right to sit at the middle table as a privilege and badge of honour and, as a consequence, rarely sat anywhere else. Because a very large proportion of socializing was done at meals, this meant that freshers missed out on important opportunities to mix with the older students, and a clear hierarchy was built into college society. When my friends and I were freshers, we felt the injustice of this keenly, and we discussed it often at mealtimes. We didn't just feel excluded, please understand; this was – we believed – a structural injustice that harmed the entire college, and once we had the power to dismantle this iniquitous and oppressive tradition, we would not hesitate to do so!

So, eventually, we became second-year students ('sophomores'). Did we campaign to bring an end to the 'middle table' tradition? We did not! Instead, we discovered that it was really quite pleasant to be able to have our meals away from the noisy freshers – they looked so young! – and to sit at the middle table with the 'seniors' and 'ladies and gentlemen' (third, fourth, and fifth-year students), who were now willing to countenance our presence. I can remember being aware of this at the time and being slightly appalled at my own behaviour. I wasn't sure whether it was just laziness or the seductive sweetness of a privilege that had previously been denied us, but one way or another, the fire in our bellies had died and we allowed the status quo to remain. Recently, I visited Perth and had a catch-up with some of these friends. In the course of our conversation, I asked the others whether they remembered this experience, and what they made of it. One member of the group had been a year behind the rest of us at college. She told me that I had been the person who had impressed upon her most strongly during her fresher year that she must not sit at the middle table. Ouch!

This small but formative experience reminds me that it can be only too human, once we find ourselves on the more comfortable end of an injustice, to develop amnesia and forget how it felt to be disadvantaged or oppressed. It also reminds me that it can be highly seductive to be admitted to a privilege from which one was once excluded. Can you remember back to a time when you experienced something similar for yourself? Were you aware of it at the time? What does it feel like to remember now? Perhaps the phenomenon we have been thinking about is what happens to Joseph here. You can perhaps imagine that it might feel wonderful to receive Pharaoh's approval and trust and to be given almost unlimited power, after years of slavery and imprisonment.

Resilience at any cost?

Joseph, of course, isn't excluding others from the privilege of sitting at the middle table in a luxurious dining hall at mealtimes. He is impoverishing the people of his adopted country to the point where they beg to be enslaved. Are his actions justified by the crisis in which he finds himself? And are they resilient? What does 'resolve' mean in this context?

I'm not disputing the assertion of the story that Joseph saved the people of Egypt and of the surrounding nations from a famine that might otherwise have destroyed them – just like the architects of Margaret Atwood's Gilead apparently 'saved' a society at threat of extinction because of rapidly declining fertility. But at what cost? When considering resilience in the context of a crisis, do the ends justify the means? Could Joseph have done something differently? Well, perhaps Joseph could have *given* grain back to the farmers who had grown it, or sold it to them for a nominal or moderate cost. Instead, Joseph took all of the people's money and gave it to his new master, Pharaoh. He took an opportunity to further ingratiate himself with Pharaoh by turning a disaster into a windfall, and by putting measures in place to ensure that the windfall would be permanent and not dry up once better conditions returned.

Does Joseph 'bounce back' from his setbacks? One would have to say that he does. Joseph had been a slave and a prisoner, and now he is second only to a king who is becoming daily more indebted to him. The result of his actions has been to improve his own situation beyond recognition. However, the impact on others has been less positive. The Egyptian people have not been destroyed by famine, but their long-term situation has been gravely diminished. Is resilience, even in a crisis situation, still resilience if it harms bystanders?

Perhaps if you think about it, you can bring to mind people or societies or nations that demonstrate striking levels of resilience in the most challenging of circumstances, but that have a tendency to damage or disadvantage others in the process.

Let me give you an example from my own background. The Barossa Valley, just outside South Australia's capital city, Adelaide, is one of the world's finest winegrowing areas. It was settled in the early 1840s, first by British immigrants and then shortly afterwards by German families escaping religious persecution in their homeland. A memorial erected in 1992 by the Barossa's German community witnesses to their thanks to God for 150 years' safe, prosperous and pious life in the beautiful Barossa. The memorial does not, however, witness to the fate of the aboriginal peoples who lived in the Barossa before the arrival of the immigrants, but who live there no longer, having been removed, more or less forcibly, by the new arrivals. The German immigrants demonstrated real resilience to escape from oppression, but they oppressed another community in the process. Curiously, something remarkably similar happened in South Africa, when French Huguenots escaped religious oppression in Holland and established the beautiful winegrowing area of Stellenbosch, inland from Cape Town. This was great for the Huguenots, but not for the native black populations, who over the ensuing centuries suffered enslavement and massacres and, eventually, apartheid.

In each case, incidentally, these new 'resilient' nations took the biblical story as their model. The memorial erected in 1992 by the German Australians (mis)quotes Joshua 2.9, 'The LORD has given us the land,' while the French Huguenots and their Afrikaner descendants saw themselves quite explicitly as 'the chosen people of the southern hemisphere', celebrating annually a covenant between themselves and God, just like God's covenant made with Israel at Sinai, on 17 December, the anniversary of the great victory of 464

Afrikaners over 10-15,000 Zulus, which proved that God was 'on their side' (although the Afrikaners' guns might also have had something to do with it . . . !). Later in South Africa's history, the Dutch Reformed Church looked to biblical texts (Gen. 1.28, the Tower of Babel story and the Pentecost story in Acts) to support the principle of 'separate development', or what we know as apartheid.

In both cases, a group of people that had suffered religious oppression demonstrated the ability to reframe (building a new identity in another hemisphere), recruit (mass emigration and resettlement is not possible without significant co-operation from others in both countries) and resolve (emigrating, alone or in company, is a complicated undertaking, as I know from hard-won personal experience). Both groups resettled successfully (at least from their own point of view) and for the long term. Today, the Barossa retains a strong German character, and the South African cricket team is full of players with French surnames! But resettlement in both cases had negative consequences for their new neighbours, and both groups morphed from being oppressed to being oppressors. Does this somehow negate what would otherwise be described as a resilient response to oppression? In principle, I can't see that it does. Resilience is an essentially self-focused concept. One is either resilient or not, without recourse to questions about how the resilience of one impacts on the experience of others.

I do have an important reservation to add, however, and it relates most closely to the element of recruitability. It is essentially the qualification that I added to the proposition in the last chapter that recruiting behaviour could be resilient even if manipulative. Human beings tend, in general, to flourish when they are in love and harmony with their neighbours. It is easier, more pleasurable and more readily sustainable to live in close contact with neighbours who are well-disposed toward us, or at least benign, than living among enemies. From time to time, however, greed or shortage or a sense of entitlement or the desire for power mean that groups of people decide to compete with their neighbours, rather than share resources (such as land), and they are willing to tolerate poor relations in exchange for greater power, wealth or territory. Especially in a situation of shortage, this *can* be highly resilient behaviour, especially in the short term, even when it significantly disadvantages others. However, over time regimes that are built on oppression and fear tend to crumble as a result of internal power struggles or because of overthrow by outsiders or by the oppressed group. In other words, while behaviour that damages others may be highly resilient in the short to medium term, it tends to be more difficult to sustain in the long term. Of course, simply exterminating your neighbours may be a way of avoiding these long-term dangers...

If we think about Joseph's behaviour just within the confines of the book of Genesis, his resilience appears clear. He recovers from terrible oppression and betrayal to become the right-hand man to a mighty king, and he uses his advantage to build reconciliation with his family. In Viktor Frankl's terms, he does what he has to do, *whatever it takes*. If we think about Joseph's behaviour as part of the sweep of the larger set of stories, of which Genesis is a part, however, it looks different. One of the first things that the reader learns upon venturing into the pages of Exodus is that a new Pharaoh has arisen – one who knows not Joseph. The reader rejoins the story at a point at which everything has been reversed. It is now not the Egyptians, but Joseph's people, the Israelites, who are enslaved. The Israelites have grown strong and multiplied, but this very growth has led to their abasement at the hands of the Egyptians, who find their growing numbers and strength threatening. In a sense, one can hardly blame the Egyptians. They have experienced both sides of the slave-master relationship and discovered that the role of master is by far the more appealing. And perhaps we should not be surprised by the dramatic reversal, for it is merely the trauma cycle continuing to influence actions and fortunes. Joseph is betrayed by his brothers and sold into slavery. When he escapes, he responds by enslaving the people of his new home for his own gain. When *they,* in turn, recover, they return the favour – enslaving and oppressing the Israelites.

We know, of course, that later in Exodus God hears the oppressed cries of his chosen people in slavery in Egypt and delivers them, bringing them out of that country and into their own land – a land flowing with milk and honey. That turns out to be a great thing for the Israelites, but not so great for the nations already living in that land, as God promises to expel or exterminate the nations (or instructs the Israelites to do so – see Deuteronomy, Judges and Joshua, for rather different takes on this part of the story). Exactly how much of the conquest story told in those books is a reflection of a massacre that actually occurred, and how much an aspirational story of a small nation seeking to make its mark in the world is unclear, but the story is nevertheless reflective of the trauma cycle making its relentless progress onwards.

The trauma cycle today

Of course, we see a similar cycle at work today, and not only in the faux-Oxbridge dining halls of university residential colleges! This same cycle continues to work itself out, not only in churches, families and communities, but also in nations. Australian politicians, for example, continue to be singly fixated on preventing new immigrants arriving by boats and on administering inhumane punishment to those who manage to get through, as a deterrent to others. Meanwhile, South Africa, which gloriously achieved the overthrow of apartheid, is now struggling with the growing corruption and oppressive behaviours of its new rulers. Archbishop Desmond Tutu used to say that the ANC managed to halt the corruption gravy-train just long enough to climb on it. And I've already suggested that something along these lines appears to be happening in feminist movements, when certain women, freed from discrimination and sexual harassment, seem to become intent upon turning older white males into their victims.

Archbishop Tutu has also, controversially, identified new instances of apartheid outside South Africa. Ironically, this includes, most prominently, Joseph's homeland, Israel. We have already traced some of the trauma cycle through the history of *ancient* Israel, seeing how Joseph's treatment at the hands of his brothers seemed to work itself out in his imprisonment and his enslavement of the Egyptians, leading, in turn, to their enslavement of the Israelites and the Israelites' expulsion of the nations from Canaan. The same cycle, sadly, is evident in modern Israel. The modern nation of Israel has suffered the most unimaginably grievous and protracted traumas, and tragically, the impact of that history now seems to be playing itself out between Israel and her neighbours, most particularly the Palestinians.

Chosen trauma

In Chapter Three we saw the steps that Joseph took to re-invent himself as an Egyptian, and we considered the importance of flexibility around retelling one's story for rebuilding personal identity following incidents of trauma, and indeed after any major life event. The same principles, it turns out, hold good for nations and other large groups.

Large groups have corporate identities, just as individuals have personal ones. Vamik Volkan, who has worked extensively in areas of intractable dispute between ethnic groups in areas such as the Balkans, the Middle East and Africa, has coined the term 'large-group identity'. He observes that individuals with whom he has worked in the context of these disputes seemed to possess two separate layers of identity, or 'garments'. The first of these layers is personal identity, and it fits the wearer like a glove. The second or outer layer Volkan describes as a loose canvas, like a tent that houses a large group. This canvas tends to be 'held up' by a leader who acts like a kind of tent pole. People wear these two garments – their individual and group identities – all the time, Volkan says, without particularly noticing them. They really only become aware of them when something goes wrong. We've already seen how this works for individuals, but it also works for large groups (or nations). When a nation regresses (suffers a major setback, including war, natural disaster, etc.), its loose canvas garment comes into the collective consciousness, and individuals make sustained efforts to repair the canvas. The greater the stress conditions, the more effort individuals will devote to this task. If the stress is extreme, then group members will feel entitled to do anything, however masochistic or sadistic, to protect their shared group identity and will rally around a charismatic leader to facilitate and encourage this effort.

Compounding this tendency is the fact that when large groups are unable to mourn the consequence of extreme events, including loss of lives, land or sovereignty, *they transmit the trauma to succeeding generations.* Not only can a large group experience trauma independently of the individuals involved, it can also pass it on to a new set of individual group members. Unresolved trauma will continue to reside in a large group even when every single one of the people who experienced the original traumatic event has died or moved on. (Yes, it's a bit like the sand dune analogy – unfortunately, group trauma can be *highly* resilient.) The damaged group identity will be unconsciously 'deposited' into the group's children as if those children were able to heal the trauma by mourning or resolving it. (This process is just like the compulsion to repeat in individuals. Trauma response, whether in individuals or groups, is 'pre-programmed' to do whatever it can to achieve its own resolution.) If the children cannot resolve the trauma, they in turn will 'deposit' it into their own children. We have seen this phenomenon play itself out clearly in some of the countries that I've already mentioned, such as South Africa and modern Israel. Volkan, who has extensive experience of working with conflict in the Balkans, calls this 'chosen trauma'. Over time, he says, the 'chosen trauma' changes its function. Group members become less focused on the details of the event itself and more focused on the way in which the memory of the event functions to knit the group, and its shared identity, together. The chosen trauma gets 'woven' into the group canvas. It may sit there dormant for years or generations, but be revived in the event of a new extreme stressor or by charismatic leaders who wish to use it for their own purposes.

Very often, a large group will observe anniversaries of such traumas; I'm thinking, for example of the surprising yet growing popularity among young people of Remembrance Day in England and of Anzac Day (commemorating the disastrous Gallipoli landings in 1915) in Australia and New Zealand. Such observances help to bind groups together. However, when a chosen trauma is involuntarily re-activated by a new trauma, the full effects of the chosen trauma come into play. Time 'collapses', and the group will feel as though the event behind the chosen trauma is happening in the here and now. The response to the new trauma may seem to outsiders to be grossly disproportionate or unduly violent. Group members themselves may even be surprised at the strength of their own reactions – but they will likely be too overwhelmed by emotion to distinguish clearly between event and feeling.

The more I discover all of this, the more it seems to make sense of modern Israel for me. Those who are not Israeli or Jewish struggle to understand both the actions of the State of Israel vis-à-vis its near neighbours and the strength and vehemence of Jewish bodies outside Israel in their opposition to anti-Semitism. Surely, I want to object, it must be possible to be critical of the actions of the modern State of Israel without being accused of being anti-Semitic? Volkan's work, however (and I should add that his is not a lone voice, merely one of the most prominent), suggests that what significant numbers of today's Israelis and Jews are experiencing whenever a Palestinian lobs a grenade or fires a rocket over the borders of the State of Israel or somebody attacks a synagogue in Britain is *the holocaust* – as if it were happening right now, even if they are too young to have been there or to have lost close family.

How extraordinary, then, that the effects of chosen trauma are written into the history of Ancient Israel. The idea of the inter-generational transmission of collective trauma is foundational to the Joseph story. I wouldn't want to suggest that the scribes who wrote the story had any idea of the theory of collective trauma, although they may, perhaps, have observed its impact. In any event, Joseph's enslavement of the people of Egypt in Genesis 47.13–26 eventually plays out its inevitable consequences in the book of Exodus. As the numbers and strength of the Israelites grow, the Egyptians become more and more afraid, and they enslave the Israelites, giving them increasingly oppressive tasks to perform and controlling numbers through the slaughter of male children (Exodus 1).

Resilience as team sport

You could be forgiven for thinking that I've painted a disastrous and inevitably doomed outlook for human societies. Certainly, you will probably be able to think of any number of intractable internecine disputes that seem to have been running forever and to which no obvious resolution seems to be presenting itself. These disputes may change and morph, as a group begins to see the face of its old enemy in a new enemy; nevertheless, the fuel of the conflict will be an event from the (distant) past. Is there something that can be done?

Well, collective trauma is very like individual trauma in this regard as well. The same sorts of responses to trauma and strate-gies for resilience also work for large groups. In the most immediate sense, opportunities to mourn and to resolve, or mediate, ongo-ing disputes are invaluable. The best way to deal with trauma is to acknowledge it, to respond to it with kindness and to give it the space and time for it to heal or to subside to some degree. The three

R's – recruiting, retelling and resolve – still hold, and trauma can be resolved sooner or it can be resolved later (by subsequent generations, just with more casualties).

The stories that a large group tells about itself will be a crucial predictor of the extent to which it continues to experience trauma and the extent to which it directs violent trauma response at others. Retelling, therefore, is an especially valuable skill. As the name 'chosen trauma' suggests, nations do get some degree of choice about how they store, shape and tell their stories. Vamik Volkan is careful to say that he doesn't necessarily mean to imply that large groups make a conscious choice to weave a past trauma prominently into their group canvases. It is something that can, and usually does, happen unconsciously. Some groups do, however, work hard to keep past traumas at the forefront of their consciousness. To what extent do days of remembrance like Blood River Day in South Africa, Anzac day in Australia and New Zealand – or even the observance of Holocaust Memorial Day – not only remember past tragedies but foster present anger and future conflicts? In one of my favourite novels, *The Sparrow*, Mary Doria Russell has one of her characters observe that when Serbs begin to become concerned that they are forgetting a grievance against a neighbour, they write an epic poem about it and require their children to recite it each evening after dinner!

This observation is borne out in real-life events, as Volkan's work with Serbians shows. In 1371 Lazar Hrebeljanovic was elected leader of Serbia. Lazar's execution was ordered during the Battle of Kosovo, and his body was mummified and entombed in a monastery, but later moved to a grave near Belgrade. Lazar was canonized, and over time the Battle of Kosovo became the Serbs' chosen trauma – stories of the battle and of Lazar were handed down from generation to generation. In the lead-up to the six hundredth anniversary of the battle, Slobodan Milosevic and his supporters decided to bring Lazar's body out of 'exile'. They took it on a tour of Serbia, visiting every village and town, where it was met by crowds of mourners and religious leaders, crying and wailing, as though the Battle of Kosovo had happened only the previous day, and swearing never to allow such a defeat to be suffered again. Milosevic was successful in his aim of reactivating the chosen trauma of the Battle of Kosovo and thus igniting a renewed Serbian nationalism. In fact, he was probably more successful than he'd intended, also igniting a new sense of entitlement to revenge for the ancient defeat, but he nevertheless continued to stir up nationalist fervour. The rest is history.

The kinds of stories that nations tell about themselves matter, and a good healthy story – one not based on victimhood – can do much to heal trauma and to build a strong, but supple and outward-looking, national identity.

My country of birth, Australia, has recently been experiencing an identity crisis that has become known as 'The History Wars'. Public awareness of identity was raised following the publication of a history of Britain's colonization of Australia, and the ongoing debate has centred upon the impact of colonization upon Aboriginal and Torres Strait Islander peoples in Australia. Former Australian Prime Minister, John Howard, waded into the previously mostly academic debate, declaring that Australia would not adopt a 'black armband' view of its own history and needed to look to its identity in a multicultural future. The debate, however, is not over, and Australia's future and the welfare of its indigenous populations, in particular, will depend in a very real sense on the 'story' that the nation eventually adopts. Meanwhile, in a delicious irony, the Australian navy patrols one of the longest coast-lines in the world to stop any more people arriving in boats!

What is the story *your* country tells about itself? One way of approaching formation of a response to this question is to ask, 'when does our history begin?' This might tell you some surprising things about which people's stories are deemed worth telling. Once you have an answer to that question, you can think about the kinds of stories your homeland tells. So, for example, does your country rely on 'chosen trauma' or 'chosen glory' to build an identity that binds the population together? Does your nation, or a substantial subset of it, tell a story of victimhood? Do you have an indigenous population(s)? Who tells their story? What do you think the health of your country's stories is and what kind of future do you think they might point to?

What of the biblical story?

There is, of course, no one single biblical story. Nevertheless, the story of Israel's salvation from slavery in Egypt and safe passage to its own land in Canaan has continued to be the principal model of salvation for modern Israel and for many other nations – as can be seen not only in the story of the Huguenots/Afrikaners, but also in the corresponding rise of black 'liberation' theologies in South Africa and elsewhere. In Jewish and Zionist imaginations, the Exodus story continues to be prominent and to be recalled and memorialized, much as Jesus' last supper is remembered and re-enacted in the Eucharist. One of the great ideas of the Hebrew Bible is that slavery was a centrally important experience for Israel – 'vouchsafed' for them by their God in order that they might know what it is to be oppressed and a stranger in the land, and, consequently, that they might devote their energy to promoting the well-being of the stranger and opposing oppression. The Israelites are instructed repeatedly in Deuteronomy, in particular, to remember that they were slaves in Egypt and therefore to follow the Torah.

This is, indisputably, a great – even a beautiful – idea. It is an idea that I find intensely painful to challenge. Nevertheless, challenge it I must. I think that it is an idea that risks perpetuating trauma. And I suspect that Palestinians are likely to agree with me. A national story that focuses on an experience of victimhood is not a healthy story and may impact negatively on the nation's neighbours. A nation that is able to reframe a story that focuses on victimhood, however, so that it becomes instead a story of training for service to the world may be able to overcome its trauma and be a positive player on the world stage. I fear that the evidence is growing that modern Israel's trauma legacy has been too great and that it is currently unable successfully to make this shift. Protracted and bloody conflict with Palestine is the result.

The Exodus story is not, however, ancient Israel's only formative story. In *Abraham: A journey* I did my best to present the story of Abraham and his descendants as an alternative biblical model for living alongside the peoples of other nations. Abraham does not bring a traumatic backstory to his journey to Canaan, and when he arrives in Canaan, he finds it full of people and does his best to get on with living alongside them. He doesn't always get it right – in fact, sometimes he makes a right pig's ear of it – but his inclination is to be a good neighbour: paying tithes to foreign priests (Genesis 14), offering hospitality to strangers (Genesis 18), interceding on behalf of other nations (Genesis 18, 20) and insisting on paying full price for land (Genesis 23). God's call to Abraham is to be a blessing to others, not to expel others from a land promised to him and his family alone. I have argued in *Abraham: A journey* and also in Chapter Three of this book that Genesis is like a kind of prequel, stuck in front of Exodus, that unsettles and challenges the Exodus paradigm. Perhaps Abraham's was a story told to counter the impact of the Exodus and Conquest stories. We'll never know. What we do know is that biblical tradition presents a multiplicity of stories to model and guide our living – and the stories we choose can have a profound effect on both ourselves and others, for good and for ill.

Resolve revisited

Where does all that leave us in terms of thinking about resolve as a factor of resilience? I think that it is difficult for us to avoid the conclusion that behaviour can be labelled 'resilient' even though it may be abusive of others. We so keenly want resilience to be good, kind, legal, edifying and *nice*. Resilience may be none of these things. Resilience may be unattractively self-focused, manipulative, damaging, and *necessary for survival*. When thinking about resolve, Frankl's work shows us that context is everything. What may be resilient in the horrors of Auschwitz may simply be unacceptable in another (perhaps any other) context. When survival is at stake, just about anything may be justified. If the context is one of thriving rather than surviving, however, the same measures, no matter how resilient, may be beyond the pale. When people's lives are at stake – in addition to the lives of others around them – then, unless one is a saint, all bets are off. In other circumstances, a person's actions will be liable to being judged on the basis of their impact on the well-being of others.

This shouldn't mean, however, that resolve should be disregarded. Flexibility might be at the heart of what it means to be resilient, but resolve also plays its role. Especially for Christians, resolve is important, as well as raising important questions about the impact of our actions upon others. Frankl's experience also has some important lessons for Christians about vocation. It suggests that having a strong sense that what I choose to be and do is not merely my own choice but something to which I am called by God is likely to increase my level of resilience, helping me to survive, thrive and achieve my goals. Frankl's experience also reminds us that when we are in the centre of a crisis, it is not the time to engage in theological questioning – it is the time to recommit to our vocation, the one that lets us know that we are engaged in the work of the kingdom.

And Gilead?

At the beginning of this chapter, I wrote about Margaret Atwood's novel, *The Handmaid's Tale*, and her imagined dystopian society, Gilead. After reading this chapter, you may feel that you have a clearer idea of what is going on in this fictional future society. Gilead is facing a trauma. A dramatic decline in fertility is challenging the very existence of the large group. Individuals come forward to find a community-based solution that can help to keep the community alive and, ideally, to build its collective identity. The story that it explicitly chooses to weave into its tent canvas is the story of Jacob, his wives, their maids and their collective children, of whom Joseph, of course, is one. We don't know what other chosen trauma, buried in the history of Gilead, might have been lying dormant, only to be reactivated by the fertility crisis. It is *possible*, of course, that the upper echelons of Gilead society are every bit as self-entitled and brutal as they appear on the surface to be, and that they have engineered or exaggerated the fertility crisis in order to bolster their own claims to power and control. An even more chilling reading of the story, however, is that they are simply ordinary people, responding to a crisis and, in the process, acting out buried prior traumas that they themselves have not known, but that have been bequeathed to them by their forebears. And just to put the 'icing' on that chilling reading, I suggested at the beginning of this chapter that these ordinary people, and their society, were displaying resilience in developing a new model for society, however brutal, that helped it to survive a crisis, which threatened its very existence.

The effects of trauma on large groups or nations can, as we have seen, be devastating. Although in today's world we are becoming increasingly attuned to the need for resilience for both individuals and groups, we do not routinely figure in and have compassion for the long-term impact of trauma. Nor do we necessarily take into account the possible impact of previous trauma experience on the outlook of those who demand resilience from others. What does a more aware and compassionate resolve look like, and how can we build our own resilience without going on to use it to oppress or terrorize others? These will be the questions for the final chapter.

6

The blessings

GENESIS 47.27—50.26

Dear Meg

We are delighted to be confirming the verbal offer made to you
and look forward to working with you.

It was nine o'clock on a Tuesday morning, and I was fast asleep when
the phone rang. I'd had a bit of an unsettled night after the latest job
interview. I had thought that the interview had gone super, super
well, but there had been no call to say I'd got the job, so I'd gone to
bed exhausted and slightly depressed at the prospect of having to
begin the recovery process all over again. I'd done my best to keep on
reminding myself that it rains almost every day in Manchester, but
even so I'd still got my hopes up about working there – way, way too
far up for my own good. So I was feeling a bit dark when I was woken
by our regular 9 a.m. automated phone call telling us that we have a
problem with our Microsoft account (I'm a Mac user).

Except that it wasn't fake-Microsoft – it was a real person, and she
was asking to speak to me! Poor old R., whose birthday it happened
to be, was then cast aside while I spent half an hour talking gleefully
to my prospective new boss, looking at calendars and hearing about
the intricacies of timetables and staff meetings. It was to be a full-time
job, it was permanent and they really wanted me – I couldn't believe it!

I'm very happy to be able to report that R. didn't mind a jot. When
I finally returned to him, beaming from ear to ear and hastily apolo-
gizing for abandoning him on his birthday, he assured me that a new

job for me was the best birthday present I could possibly have given him. We proceeded to have a wonderful day – a real birthday day. We caught a slow boat up the Thames, and I borrowed a wheelchair and walked him around Kew Gardens before finishing up with a pub meal. The sun shone, and a bit of drizzle fell, and we had a wonderful time talking non-stop about our new life – happy and relieved finally to have some kind of an idea what that new life might look like. We had done so much imagining of potential future lives (always having to check our emotions in case we got too attached to them) in cities as diverse as Edinburgh, Durham (UK *and* USA), Oslo and Brisbane, that finally to know that Manchester was to be the city that would be our next home was a wonderful feeling – precipitation levels notwithstanding.

Resilience and happy endings

So, I have to confess that I'm feeling a little nervous about your reaction to my good news. I'm nervous that if you've read *Abraham: A journey*, you might be rolling your eyes at this point and thinking to yourself 'here we go – another happy ending.' 'We don't all get happy endings!' you might be thinking. Even if you didn't read *Abraham: A journey,* you may be wondering whether a happy ending is quite the best way to finish a book about resilience?

Well, all I can say is that this is the ending I got, and we are all just going to have to deal with it. I had no idea how my job search would end when I started this book. In fact, I still had no idea three quarters of the way through the last chapter! All the while I've been writing, I've been wondering how this part of my story would work out and what kind of a story it would turn out to be. Just how much resilience would I have to develop, and how much reframing would I have to do in order to be able to carry on?

You see, over the course of writing this book, my life fell apart a little bit. Ironically, it was while I was working on the theory of trauma.

Apparently, it is not at all unusual for people who are engaged in working with trauma to find themselves experiencing it.

You might have noticed the reference to a wheelchair when I was talking about Kew Gardens. R. has had – and so we both have had – an extremely tough year. The worst of either of our lives. He has been unwell and unable to go to work for 12 months, and during that time, I have been his carer. It has absolutely given me a renewed sense of respect for people who care for their loved ones long term. We are hopeful that R.'s health will improve dramatically and that we will soon be able to give wheelchairs the shove, but he has had to take early retirement and our lives have changed completely. So, you see, my job search recently got a whole lot more serious and a whole lot more pressured. My short-term job working on the trauma project came to an end, and we found ourselves facing an uncertain future in which both of us were unemployed and homeless. Along the way, we had to call in a few favours and follow up a few fallback positions. When even our fallback positions started falling through, we began to be disillusioned, starting to doubt ourselves and wondering whether there was any kind of future for us. Manchester hasn't come a moment too soon.

So, you might be reacting to my happy ending in a number of different ways, perhaps depending on where you are in your own journey. My good fortune – my blessings – may be encouraging you to hope that yours are also on their way. On the other hand, you may feel that hope of that kind is difficult or dangerous for your peace of mind, and that you don't need to be reminded of others' good fortunes. A journey requiring resilience can go on for a very, very long time and be extremely draining. My job hunt, in the end, lasted six years – but I know that journeys requiring resilience can last for so long that they can make six years seem like a sprint.

Happy endings come in all sorts of shapes and sizes. Very often, as you no doubt already know, they don't usually involve precisely the thing you were hoping for. Sometimes they involve something better than you were hoping for, but very often they are about learning to look back and see that where we have got to is not such a bad place after all. Sometimes a simple reframing exercise – looking at things in a new framework – can be enough to turn an unhappy ending into a happy one.

How does Joseph's story end up? Is it a happy or unhappy ending? And has he learned resilience? It is time to find out.

Jacob's blessings

In Chapter Five the focus was all on Joseph's dealings with the Egyptians – here, we return to the place where we began, the story of Joseph's relationships with his father and brothers. At the very end of Genesis 47, we learn that Jacob and his family settle in the land of Goshen and are fruitful and multiply there exceedingly. In the next verses the authors do some quite significant 'reframing'.

Even though the story and the people have moved to Egypt (and must do so if the end of Genesis and the beginning of Exodus are to appear seamless), Jacob the ancestor must 'rest', finally, with his ancestors in Canaan. So, Genesis 47.29 tells the reader that as Jacob's days are ending, he calls Joseph to his bedside and asks him to swear to carry his bones to Canaan for burial in the ancestral burial cave that Abraham bought from the Hittites. Joseph agrees. In Jacob's request he uses some words and phrases that remind the attentive reader of Abraham's search for a wife for Isaac (e.g. 'put his hand under [Jacob's] thigh' and to 'promise to deal loyally and truly with [Jacob])' and by repeating these phrases the author helps to build the sense that Canaan is at the very centre of the story, even though the characters have taken a detour, for the moment, south to Egypt.

The reframing continues at the beginning of Chapter 48. Joseph is told that Jacob is ill, and so he takes his (Joseph's) sons, Manasseh and Ephraim, to meet Jacob before his death. When Jacob hears that Joseph has come to him, he sits up in bed and recites for Joseph the blessing given to him by God in Luz, in Canaan. It is purportedly the blessing given to him in Genesis 35 (along with the new name 'Israel' – Gen 35.10), but Jacob in fact puts together bits from three different 'blessing' passages:

> I will make you fruitful and increase your numbers. I will make you an assembly of peoples, and I will give this land to your seed as an everlasting possession. (Gen. 48.4)

This 'remembered blessing' draws together elements of the blessings and promises made to Jacob first in Genesis 28 and later in Genesis 34, with the promise of the land as a 'perpetual holding' (the Hebrew is the same as the Hebrew translated 'everlasting possession' in Genesis 48.4) made to Abraham in Genesis 17.8. Jacob's speech also suggests that these promises have been fulfilled by God. To explain why that is so requires some quite technical discussion that you might find interesting, or perhaps just tedious. If you would like to read it, you'll find it in Appendix 1. You could read it there now, or just keep on reading here and come back to it later (or not).

This reframing is important for at least two reasons. At one level the authors are constructing a 'framework' across the ancestral narratives of Genesis that binds them all together and that creates a coherent set of promises that travels with them. At another level, however, the authors are rewriting the story of Israel, so that it is a new and hopeful one that has 'somewhere to go' in terms of helping to move the Israelites into the future.

In Chapter Three I talked about the ways in which the biblical writers reframed Israel's story both after the exile and after the return from exile. I suggested that they had to confront their concerns about the future and find ways to live with what appeared to be the failure, or the end, of God's promises: Israel was very small in comparison with some of its neighbours, the Temple was in ruins, there was no descendant of David on the throne, and Israel had 'lost' the land given to her by YHWH. A number of different reframing approaches were employed. The largest-scale piece of reframing involved a bit of narrative 'rearrangement'. At the very core of Israel's story had been the first six books (or 'Hexateuch'): Genesis, Exodus, Leviticus, Numbers, Deuteronomy and Joshua. These six books told Israel's story: the period of the ancestors, delivery from slavery in Egypt, the wandering in the wilderness, the giving of the Torah at Sinai and, finally, the conquest of Canaan. Israel's story was one of suffering and salvation through divine gift of law and land. After the exile and disappointing return to Canaan, however, the returners appeared to have lost the land (even once they had returned, they found that their homes, businesses, and land had been taken over by others) and to have proven themselves to be incapable of keeping the law. What to do?

In their biggest single piece of reframing, the biblical authors cut off the ending to the story. They just got rid of Joshua from the 'core' books, leaving five books (or 'Pentateuch'). This group of books became authoritative as the 'Torah', while Joshua became part of a larger collection often called the 'Deuteronomistic History' (Joshua – 2 Kings). 'What difference does *that* make?' you might ask! Actually, a lot. Whereas the Hexateuch ended with the glorious conquest of Canaan, at the end of the new 'Pentateuch', the Hebrews are poised on the very edge of the promised land, about to enter it. They are a people for whom the glorious promises are all ahead – all in the future. The promises cannot have been broken *because they have not yet been fulfilled*. This story of 'waiting' becomes the Israelites' new story and a crucial part of their new identity. Rather than a people who had been given God's promised gifts and squandered them, they styled themselves as 'the people of the promise', whom God had chosen and who lived permanently on the verge of coming into God's chosen future. The 'promise' became everything. As part of that, a 'new' web of promises was woven into Genesis. Because these 'new' promises were set in the distant past, it was possible to see that they hadn't been tarnished or broken by the destruction of Jerusalem and the exile. Here were fresh promises for Israel to live with and through, into the future.

Reframing as competitive sport

I've already talked, however, about there being a number of different 'voices' in the Joseph story. So, for example, we've seen one voice backing Joseph to take over the mantle from Jacob and another backing Judah. Many scholars hear several different voices 'speaking' through Genesis, engaged in several different exercises of reframing at the same time. Scholars hypothesize about these voices and the theologies or ideologies behind them, even trying to match them up with particular groups or 'schools' of people. Often there is very persuasive evidence to back up these hypotheses, sometimes not so much. Many scholars associate the web of texts I referred to above (including Genesis 17; 24; 28; 34—35 and 48) with a Priestly school, or 'P'. The idea that some of the writing has a priestly character or can be attributed to a source called 'P' is one of the strongest of these hypotheses. If 'P' means something to you, great – if not, it doesn't matter. What is important is that it is a voice doing some reframing of the story.

The reframing that P does goes a step further than even the large reframing exercise I've just described – the one that makes Israel 'the people of the promise', with fulfilment always just around the corner. For P, the promises have *already* been fulfilled – however, they don't mean what everyone had always assumed they meant. For P, the promises take on a new, more universalist aspect (a bit like the portrait of YHWH in Genesis 1–2.4a, which is also P). Let's see if I can explain that, using the three promises that Jacob talks about in his 'remembered blessing' in Genesis 48.3–4. The fulfilment of the promise to make Jacob 'fruitful' and to 'increase him' is indicated by Genesis 47.27: 'Thus Israel settled in the land of Egypt, in the region of Goshen; and they gained possessions in it, and were fruitful and multiplied exceedingly'. The promise to make Jacob an 'assembly of peoples' is fulfilled, at least symbolically, through the allusion to the twelve tribes of Israel in Jacob's blessings of his sons in Genesis 49.

I want to say something a little more about the third promise – the promise to give 'this land' to 'Jacob's seed as an everlasting possession'. In the old story that still had Joshua tacked on to the end, the promise of land was an exclusive promise – it required the Israelites to remove all of the former residents from the land before they could inhabit it. This is a little like the understanding of ownership of land that we have today, in which the holder of the title is entitled to exclude other people from their land and have the sole enjoyment of it. P's concept of land ownership is different. For P, 'ownership of land' entitles the 'owner' to use it in a way rather like we understand leases. For P, God was the title holder of all the land, and the promise of land to Abraham and his descendants was a bit like the granting of an open-ended lease – except that God reserved the right to grant multiple leases to single pieces of land! In other words, the gift of the land, for P, was the gift of the right to live in and enjoy the land, *alongside those who were already there.* All of the references to God's promise to give the land to Abraham, Isaac and Jacob and their descendants throughout Genesis, when put together, show that this gift has already been made. P supports its understanding of land ownership by having God instruct Abraham and his descendants to live in the land as 'aliens' or 'sojourners' (*gerim*) alongside the other nations already there. I said more about this in *Abraham: A journey.*

Are you getting a sense of how P's reframing works? (There's more, but that's enough for the moment!) Imagine the Israelites returning from exile in sophisticated Babylon. While there, they were surrounded by peoples of many, many nations. Possibly they found that working together was a savvy, or at least pragmatic, way of getting on. When they arrive home, they find it is a case of *plus ça change.* Their land, too, is now full of people from many lands (including

Israelites who never left) – people living in their houses, working their land and businesses, worshipping a panoply of gods. P's reframing is a way of responding to this. P tells an identity story that says 'Israel is a nation chosen and blessed by YHWH *to live alongside others* and to mediate YHWH's blessings to them'. You can see how this is different from the previous story which said that 'Israel was chosen and blessed by YHWH to be 'top dog' and subdue or even exterminate other nations.' This new sense of what it meant to be given the land by God, along with a new vocation of living with neighbours, gave Israel a way forward, because it told a story in which Israel had *not* lost the land, and in which relationship with YHWH could truly be everlasting.

You're probably getting a sense that there are quite a few cooks with a hand in this broth – or rather, quite a lot of groups doing reframing here all at once! There are. I've given you just one example. But what is really extraordinary about it is that the authors of the Pentateuch allowed many stories to sit alongside one another. They didn't replace the old with the new, or choose between two different takes on the story. They all have a place, even if they're jostling with one another for prominence. That has quite an impact, I think, on how we read the Bible. What do you think?

Going back home

There was a while there when I thought that my story was going to turn out a little like Jacob's – going back home for burial. (Well, in my case 'burial' might be putting it a *little* strongly.) Six years ago, I set out on my Awfully Big Adventure to travel to the UK and get married. Even just a few weeks before I got the Manchester job, I thought it looked like it was time for me to go home again to Australia. I wasn't finding work, R. was retiring, and I just needed to find *something*. I wasn't homesick, but I had seen enough of the UK/Europe/USA academic job markets to know that it was pretty unlikely that I was going to find long-term work in a hurry. Actually, so certain was I that R. and I were going to return home to Australia that I very nearly didn't apply for Manchester.

Eighteen months or so previously, an old boss had made me an open promise about trying to find work for me if ever we were to return to Australia. R. and I had resisted the idea, turning it into our 'fallback position', but eventually we reached the stage when it was time to explore – gratefully – this option. I anticipated that it might feel a bit like going home with my tail between my legs – a bit like failure. However, I know about reframing! I decided that it would be fine, and that if it wasn't fine, then I would make it fine. We would be going back to live in Brisbane, where R. and I were married, and that was something I could get excited about. You see, I have much-loved friends in Brisbane, but more to the point (sorry, dear ones), an ordinary winter's day in Brisbane can be sunny with a maximum of 23 degrees! Any Australian who has lived through a London winter or two (or a Manchester winter or two) will know that that sounds like paradise. I persuaded myself that winter weather of the Brisbane kind was all I needed to make me perfectly happy for the rest of my life. I would make the most of it by buying a luxury flat, towering above the Brisbane River, with access to an infinity pool. (See how we suffer in the Lord's service! Well, somebody has to minister to people who live in nice climates, surely?)

Yes, it was going to be great. You'll have worked out by now, of course, that it didn't happen. Encouraged by many colleagues, R. and I went to Brisbane to get the lie of the land and, we hoped, to put together a picture of what this new work for me, or for both of us, would look like. It started out well. The winter weather was duly warm, and it was wonderful to see friends. We explored and imagined. Then, without warning, on the final day of the trip, the whole thing fell into a heap, and it became apparent that, due to a series of entirely well-meaning misunderstandings, there was in fact absolutely nothing for us in Brisbane – no funding, which meant no jobs, no house, no immediate prospects. Despite the various hints and ideas, we had got it wrong.

Have you ever been in the situation of slightly grudgingly opting to go with your fallback position and then watching as the fallback position falls through? It is not a comfortable feeling. We got on the plane for the 24-hour journey back to grey and chilly London with heavy hearts. I had a feeling that coming back from this one was going to be a bit of a challenge. And yet, in the middle of it all, I was aware of a tiny sense of relief that we wouldn't be leaving the UK after all and that Manchester was still a possibility. And then, on the day after we got back to London, I got an email to say that I'd been short-listed for Manchester. I didn't know whether to be relieved or terrified about going through the whole experience all over again and running the risk of yet another failure. Would I be able to bear this one?

WWGiTFY?
(Where Was God in That For You?)

One of the more curious features of this devotional book is that it has had relatively little to say about God. In all sorts of ways, that's not ideal! To a large extent, it is a reflection of the story of Joseph that has been our biblical focus. God has certainly not been absent. However, the divine has been elusive in the story. Joseph talks about God quite a bit, especially at important moments, but each time he's done so, we've expressed reservations about his piety. Is it genuine or is his humility contrived and his God-talk, in truth, just another expression of a megalomania out of control? Further, when we've considered matters such as God's presence, God's intervention in events, or God's name, we've found ourselves confronted more often by human politics than by spiritual truths.

We will need to come back to the role of God in the story a little later, but just now I want to say something about my experience. One of the things that has interested me over the last six years of my job search has been observing my lack of worry. Despite all of the setbacks and the frustrations and disappointments, and even with R.'s retirement rapidly approaching, I have never gone to bed at night worried that I might *never* find work. I have told myself, and others, that the right thing would come along just when I really needed it. And my lack of worry suggests to me that I have actually believed that. It is certainly my experience that God works in this way. Even though I might find myself in a wilderness for a very protracted period, and feeling forgotten and unable to perceive how I might ever get out of it, God seems to get into action just when needed and direct me towards something which, while not necessarily what I wanted or was looking for, turns out to be something that is good and life-giving for me.

I suspect that had the Manchester job come up six years ago, when I was first setting out on my job hunt, I might not have bothered to apply. Manchester is, after all, in the north, and it rains pretty much constantly there, and the college has neither a highly prestigious reputation nor a direct connection with my own denomination.

Well, that would have been my bad. I don't think it is that I'm now prepared to settle for something I wouldn't previously have considered seriously. It is rather that my experiences in the meantime have genuinely changed my outlook, so that I now see the true value of something I mightn't have noticed before. The fact that I won't be working for my own denomination might just turn out to be a plus – I won't have to feel a need to carry responsibility for the particular brands of weird politics that I will inevitably encounter in my work. All churches have them – but these won't be mine! And after the year that R. and I have had, getting out of London is likely to be a Very Good Thing. And prestige? You can have it. With prestige, I have learned, come politics and pressure and a lack of freedom for research and writing and really being with people. Give me keen students. More importantly, I have been offered this job on a permanent basis. That just doesn't happen in academia anymore! You know, looking back, only one or two of the positions I've applied for over the last six years has had a lifetime of longer than one, three or five years – at least without having to jump through crazy academic hoops in order to win tenure. It turns out that I got lucky. Who knew?

God knew. Yes, I am sufficiently religiously unreconstructed to believe that the hand of God has been at work in all of this, and I can now look back at all of those opportunities I talked myself into wanting so badly and say 'there, but for the grace of God'. And I can also say that the short-term job that I did find along the way – the one that wasn't really what I was looking for, but in the course of which I learned about trauma and resilience – quite possibly saved my life, and maybe R.'s life, too. Without some basic knowledge of trauma response, which allowed me to respond to my situation with understanding and compassion, rather than frustration and judgement, I don't know that we'd have survived the last year. And now there is something new for me to look forward to. Apparently, unlike Joseph, it is not yet time for my bones to be carried back home. Praise the Lord!

Does your experience of God look anything like this? Does looking back over your life give you reassurance that you don't need to worry about the things that currently seem beyond your grasp, even if they drive you crazy? No doubt your experience will differ from mine, in ways small or large. Whatever your experience has been, how does it fit with Joseph's story? Are you like me and glad that it's not yet time for your bones to be carried home? Are you at peace, finally, with the people around you and looking forward to what is coming next? Or are you like Joseph and Judah, wondering who will eventually come out on top and win the blessing? Are you feeling resilient? And, however you are or have been, WWGiTFY?

So far in this chapter we have been focused on reframing – a process with which we are now becoming increasingly familiar. We have seen how Joseph's story functions as part of a reframing exercise that helped different groups in post-exile Judah to find a new story, or stories, to tell about themselves that would help them to forge a new future – one in which their shortcomings in keeping God's covenant and laws wouldn't mean the end of God's promises to them or of the special relationship between them, through which they were building their identity.

Throughout this book we have been thinking about the ways in which we, too, need to reframe the stories through which we build our own identities. I hope that you have been able to identify times in your life when you have had to respond to new circumstances by doing a little, or a lot, of reframing. Are you facing a situation now that will require some retweaking to your story? If so, which of your identities is most occupying your attention? Is it your own personal identity or your group identity that is currently most in the forefront of your mind? As I write the first draft of this final chapter, the United Kingdom seems to be drifting further and further towards perhaps its most dramatic national crisis, as the proposed 'Brexit' date, already postponed multiple times, inches ever closer. Many of us are so focused on these developments that concerns about our own personal identities are taking a back seat. Whatever comes out of this Brexit mess (and it is a mess –.whatever your own personal views happen to be) will need some carefully focused reframing in order to allow the building of a healthy new national identity. I wonder whether it will get it? (Coming back to this chapter in a later draft, I note that although Brexit has actually, finally, happened we still don't have a much clearer idea of what it is all going to mean.)

Inheriting

But it is time to get back to Joseph. Everything that we've read in Joseph's story to this point has been leading us to what comes next – the big denouement in which it is revealed which son or sons will receive the inheritance and blessings of their dying father, Jacob. In the story, questions of inheritance are addressed prior to the death of the male parent, rather than in a will, and Chapter 49 of Genesis is almost completely comprised of the blessings that Jacob makes over his sons once he is close to death. Before we get to them, however, there is one more tiny bit of the story to deal with. Unusually, the blessings of Joseph's sons Ephraim and Manasseh are addressed *before* those of Jacob's sons. In one sense this is skipping a generation; however, you might remember from the discussion above that Jacob claimed the two boys as his own.

At this point of the story, however, it is a little more complicated. Although in many respects Jacob treats the lads as Joseph's sons, and in fact doesn't seem even to recognize them, Jacob claims the right to bless them as well as their father. Jacob first blesses Joseph and then his boys:

> The God before whom my ancestors Abraham and
>   Isaac walked,
> the God who has been my shepherd all my life to this
>   day, the angel who has redeemed me from all
>   harm, bless the boys;
> and in them let my name be perpetuated, and the
>   name of my ancestors Abraham and Isaac;
> and let them grow into a multitude on the earth.
>   (Gen. 48.15–16)

In this bit of the story, and in this blessing, Joseph is at one and the same time acknowledged as the boys' father *and* written out of history. Somehow, it is clear that the rightful ancestors of Israel are and will be Abraham, Isaac and Jacob, and that Joseph will never quite rise to the dizzying heights of ancestor. And so the blessings travel straight from Jacob to the boys.

In the meantime, we have here another story of the younger son supplanting his elder brother, the firstborn. When Jacob blesses the lads, he crosses his hands before placing them on their heads, so that his right hand is on the head of the younger, Ephraim. When Joseph objects, his father persists, saying that the elder, Manasseh, shall be great and shall become a great people, but that the younger shall be greater and that his offspring shall become a multitude of nations (Gen. 48.19, cf. Abraham in Gen. 17.4). At every stage of Genesis, then, beginning with Cain and Abel (Gen. 4.4–5), and continuing with Ishmael and Isaac, Jacob and Esau, and Leah and Rachel, the younger is chosen over the elder, confounding the culture and tradition of the time.

As we approach the penultimate chapter of the book of Genesis, there still remains one generation not fully accounted for. Even if Joseph's children have now been categorized and sorted, there are still outstanding questions about their father and his brothers. I've already suggested that in one sense Joseph has been written out of the story. And we still need to submit Joseph and his brothers to 'the sorting hat', to borrow a Potter-ism.

In Genesis there is a pattern by which the identity of 'chosen' son is marked by one (or both) of two things: blessing and inheritance. These two elements feature prominently in some of the most important plot developments in Genesis. For example, in Genesis 21 Sarah has Hagar and Ishmael sent away because she doesn't want Ishmael to inherit along with her son, Isaac. Meanwhile, in Gen 25.29–34 Esau gives his inheritance to Jacob in exchange for a bowl of stew, while in Genesis 27 Jacob tricks Esau out of his blessing. Both inheritance and blessing – are about to be dealt with in our story – inheritance first.

The inheritance of the firstborn

The law of inheritance governing situations in which a man has sons by two mothers is carefully set out in Deut. 21.15–17, which provides that the right of the firstborn son to receive a double share must be honoured whether the firstborn's mother is loved or hated by her husband, the boy's father. This prevents a man circumventing the tradition that the firstborn receives double the portion of inheritance received by his brothers, as he might be tempted to do if he 'hates' the mother of his firstborn but 'loves' the mother of one of his other sons. The authors of Genesis undoubtedly knew this *torah* when they were putting together Joseph's story. We can be confident about knowing this, because they added brief passages that correspond to Deut. 21.15–17. Way, way back in Genesis 29, there are two verses that say that Jacob loved Rachel (29.18), but hated Leah (29.33). So here we are certainly dealing with a case in which a father hates the mother of his firstborn (Reuben) and loves the mother of one of his younger children (Joseph). Jumping back now to Genesis 48, we find this:

Then Israel said to Joseph, 'I am about to die, but God will be with you and will bring you again to the land of your ancestors. *I now give to you one portion more than to your brothers*, the portion that I took from the hand of the Amorites with my sword and with my bow.' (Gen. 48.21–22)

And that's not the only allusion to Deuteronomy 21.17. In Genesis 49.3 Jacob describes Reuben as 'my firstborn, my might and the first fruits of my vigour' and the Hebrew of this phrase is precisely the Hebrew of Deuteronomy 21.17.

So, here seems to be one really important marker of Joseph's chosenness. Jacob gives a double portion to Joseph even though Joseph is not his firstborn and even though the Torah says he mustn't, *and* the text does everything it can to draw attention to Jacob's breach of Deuteronomy 21.17! In Appendix 2 you'll see some further discussion about the more mysterious aspects of Jacob's preference for Joseph and about some of the surprising links between this and other inheritance stories (including Genesis 21, in which Abraham breaches this same Torah provision by refusing to give his Egyptian son his due inheritance!) But for the moment, we can satisfy ourselves with saying that it seems that Joseph is ahead by a nose in the inheritance stakes.

Blessing of the firstborn

What about blessing? If you read the notes in Appendix 2, you'll know that the situation concerning inheritance is a little bit more complicated and ambiguous than the overview I've just given would suggest. Blessing is perhaps a little more straightforward than inheritance, but is still nuanced. Chapter 49 of Genesis is comprised entirely of Jacob's deathbed blessings of his 12 sons. The '12 sons' include Joseph, but not Joseph's two sons Manasseh and Ephraim. Most of the blessings are relatively brief. The blessings of Judah and Joseph stand out from the others because of their length. (If you haven't read them for a while, now would be a good time to look them up.)

The 'blessings' of Jacob's eldest three sons, Reuben, Simeon and Levi, are actually more like curses – they explain why the three have been excluded from consideration as Jacob's firstborn: Reuben had gone to bed with Bilhah, his father's concubine and his aunt's servant (Gen. 35.22), while Simeon and Levi had shown themselves to be men of anger and violence (Gen. 34). The next brother is Judah, and the way has been cleared for him to take on the mantle of firstborn by the elimination of the previous three.

So, does he? Judah's blessing is long and complimentary. Joseph's is also long and overwhelmingly positive. Both blessings are five verses long, although Joseph's verses are longer, so his overall blessing takes up more space on the page than Judah's.

For three reasons, however, the blessings favour Judah over Joseph and point to Judah as the 'chosen' or 'firstborn' son of his generation.

First is the simple fact that his three elder brothers are eliminated, so that he is left as the next eldest brother and therefore the most likely candidate.

The second reason why Judah is favoured is that his blessing has royal connotations, applying to him the explicit language of monarchy:

> The sceptre shall not depart from Judah,
>> nor the ruler's staff from between his feet,
> until tribute comes to him;
>> and the obedience of the peoples is his.
>> (Gen. 49.10)

This seems pretty clear – Judah is the anointed one. Further, as I said in *Abraham: A journey,* monarchic language is of particular importance in Genesis. The story of Abraham, in particular, is modelled closely on the story of David, using that story as a kind of framework for a (superficially) different story about a new, democratized world that is set in the ancient past, and which yet shares a number of the features of the world of the returning exiles from Babylon. If Judah is being presented here as a king, then that is a very strong indicator that he is to be regarded as the foremost among the brothers.

There is one further reason why Judah's blessing singles him out as the chosen brother, and it is probably the most interesting of the three. Part of the blessing appears to be designed precisely to *eclipse* Joseph. Judah's blessing begins like this:

> Judah, your brothers shall praise you;
>> your hand shall be on the neck of your
>>> enemies;
>> your father's sons shall bow down
>>> before you. (Gen. 49.8)

Wait, wasn't it *Joseph* who was supposed to have his brothers bowing down before him? This blessing, of course, recreates Joseph's dreams from the very beginning of the story, but it puts Judah in Joseph's place. We have come full circle and find ourselves back at the beginning with Joseph's dream, except that now it looks different – and it *is* different. Joseph has been sidelined – just as he was by his brothers at the beginning of the story. This, too, is reflected in the blessings. Joseph's blessing ends like this:

> The blessings of your father
>   are stronger than the blessings of the
>   eternal mountains,
>   the bounties of the everlasting hills;
> may they be on the head of Joseph,
>   *on the brow of him who was set apart*
>   *from his brothers.* (Gen. 49.26)

Incidentally, the use of royal language in Jacob's blessing of Judah contributes to this sense of the eclipse of Joseph, as royal language was also used about Joseph in the description of his dreams in Genesis 37 *and* because the final line of Genesis 49.26 points to Joseph's having the role of a judge rather than of a king. You will find more detail about the final line of Genesis 49.26, and how it does this in Appendix 3.

So, which son wins the mantle of Jacob's heir? If you were to consider only inheritance, you would probably say it was Joseph. If you were to consider only blessing, you would probably say it was Judah. The sense in the blessings, however, that Judah *eclipses* Joseph points to Judah's overall victory and also points to the eventual privileged place given to Judah the nation, over and above the Northern Kingdom, Israel, where Joseph's sons, Manasseh and Ephraim, had their ancestral lands. The residual ambiguities around both inheritance and blessing, on the other hand, bear witness to the multiple voices that speak from the text.

The deaths of Jacob and Joseph

In any event, it is Joseph who spends 40 days embalming his father, in the Egyptian manner, while the Egyptians, for their part, weep for 70 days. The family is in Joseph's country, and so Joseph takes charge. Remarkably, all of the servants of Pharaoh, the elders of his household and the elders of the land of Egypt go with Joseph and his household to Canaan to bury Jacob! Curiously, Joseph asks to go to Canaan to bury Jacob not in the traditional burial cave of his ancestors as Jacob had made Joseph swear he would do (Gen. 47.29–31; 49.29–32), but in a tomb that he says that Jacob had hewn out for himself in Canaan (Gen. 50.5). Even more curiously, Joseph then leads the caravan of Egyptians and Hebrews to the threshing floor of Atad (which is never otherwise heard of, either before or afterwards, and about which nothing is known except that it is 'beyond the Jordan' – that is, in the far northeast and *outside* Canaan [Gen. 50.10–11]) before finally burying Jacob in Abraham's burial cave back in Canaan. Strange!

There is one final postscript to the story. Once Jacob has been buried and the family has returned to Egypt, his brothers lose their collective nerve. They suddenly realize that Jacob is no longer there to be a buffer between themselves and Joseph, and they become worried that Joseph may be continuing to hold a grudge against them and that he might still seek vengeance. They make up a story that Jacob had asked them to pass on a message to Joseph, asking him to forgive 'the crime of the slaves of Elohim, your father' (Gen. 50.17). Well, Joseph weeps, his brothers weep, and then they fall down before him and declare themselves to be Joseph's slaves. (Judah might have won their father's final blessing, and that blessing might have eclipsed Joseph's dream of dominance, but Joseph gets the last laugh!)

Joseph responds to his brothers in a manner that should be familiar to us by now. He tells them that he is not in the place of God, before going on to put himself in pretty much that very place (see also Gen. 40.8; 41.15–16)! He tells his brothers that even though they had acted with the intention of harming Joseph when they faked his death and sold him to … foreign traders, God had been behind the whole thing and had meant it to be for the good of the Egyptian people. They shouldn't fear – Joseph himself would provide for them.

Joseph went on to live a long life in Egypt, and before he died, he made his brothers swear to take his bones back to Canaan. Joseph was embalmed in the Egyptian fashion and placed in an Egyptian coffin, and his story – and the book of Genesis – end with one final recital of God's promise to give the land to Abraham, Isaac and Jacob.

A strange story

When it all comes down to it, Joseph's is a strange story. Earlier I asked what kind of story it was – a comedy or a tragedy, or something in between? In some ways it is hard to say – ultimately, it is a mix of things. The Egyptians and the surrounding nations have been saved from starvation, but they have been enslaved. Joseph and his brothers have reached a kind of uneasy truce, but who knows what Joseph may have done in his final years? Meanwhile, the reader knows that Judah eventually wins the day, that the slavery of the Egyptians will re-invent itself as the slavery of the Hebrews, and that soon there will arise a Pharaoh who knows not Joseph. (Exod. 1.8)

I also wanted to know, along the way, whether Joseph would turn out to be a resilient character as we use that term today, whether or not the ancient writers would have understood it. Well, I think that one would need to say – on any measure – that he does. Even when he is finally, apparently, supplanted as his father's favourite in the context of Jacob's deathbed blessings, he doesn't give up, and the book ends with Joseph promising, in slightly superior fashion, to be the one who will provide for the rest of his family who are, once again, prostrate in front of him. There is also a (quite subtle!) hint that he is, or has become, *God's* chosen one (if not Jacob's), if the use of the noun 'nazirite' in Joseph's blessing (see the discussion in Appendix 3) is understood to link him with Samuel and Samson. If that is the case, then perhaps Joseph comes to represent the pattern of the judges (the system of rulership 'chosen' by God) rather than that of monarchy (the system of rulership 'chosen' by the people – see 1 Samuel 8).

The question of Joseph's resilience raises the larger issue of resilience itself – our theme throughout this book and the lens through which we've read Joseph's story. We've looked at resilience fairly comprehensively, exploring the three factors Reframing, Recruiting and Resolve in depth, and I hope that you feel that you have a much stronger sense of what resilience involves, and how to get it, than you had at the beginning of the book. We've also thought about the ethics of resilience. We've seen that although resilience is a terrifically good thing to have for oneself, it can be both used and abused. Abuse can occur when one 'does whatever it takes' to build up one's own resilience at the expense of another person, or demands that another person displays resilience, thus relieving oneself of the responsibility to offer care for them, or at least to offer basic levels of safety and ethical treatment.

I've come to the conclusion, I think, that resilience is morally neutral – rather like fire or stories. We need resilience if we are to live well, but it can be a bit lethal if allowed to get out of hand. It is important, even necessary, to learn resilience in order to get on in our stressful and traumatized modern world. Without it, we are unlikely to be in a position to bring the full force of our own particular contributions and gifts to the world. Christians, however, will want to consider resilience within a framework of Christian ethics of behaviour. For a Christian, one's own resilience can and must never be foremost – the quest for resilience should not be allowed to trump Jesus' injunction to love neighbour as oneself in any but situations of the greatest crisis. Joseph's story has given us the opportunity to explore not only what resilience looks like, but also its shadow side, and Joseph emerges from it as a bit of a mixed model, patterning for us both how to become resilient and also the excesses and dangers that we are well-advised to be aware of and to avoid.

And they all lived happily ever after ...

How is your relationship with Joseph at the end of all of this? With whom are your sympathies lying? I'm afraid that I haven't really gone out of my way to make Joseph your new favourite biblical character, have I? What I hope, perhaps, is that along the way you might have felt some compassion for Joseph. Hopefully, you've also felt some compassion for Joseph's long-suffering brothers, for the childless Mr and Mrs Potiphar, for the hungry, enslaved Egyptians and perhaps even for yourself, making your way through some of the longer and more technical sections! Compassion is not a bad attitude with which to counter the effects of the worst excesses of resilience – whether within others or within oneself.

I started out in this chapter being concerned about your response to my happy ending. Of course, the truth is that my new job is not an ending at all but rather a beginning. Probably in no time, I'll be missing the freedom to sleep in and write all day in cafes, or at home in my pyjamas! But I'm looking forward to being part of a community that worships together and to walking alongside people who are preparing for ministry and hearing their stories. And I'm looking forward to sharing with them the stories of Abraham and Joseph (and Sarah and Hagar and Dinah and Rebekah ...) and helping them to do some reframing in conversation with those stories. And perhaps to talking about resilience, just a little bit.

And you? Where are you now in your resilience journey? Does it help to know something of trauma and trauma response, and how are you getting on with reframing? Where does your own journey of resilience have parallels with Joseph's journey, and where do the two differ? I hope that you have taken the opportunity to use

Joseph's story as a springboard to telling and retelling your own story.

Where does your mind go now, when news reports or advertising or promotional materials for church training programmes talk about resilience? And what is the framework that will work for you in terms of avoiding resilience's worst excesses? Whether you are having your own happy ending, or your story seems to be just a little strange, or you are feeling overwhelmed by something or by everything, I wish you God's shalom on your journey. And resilience – but maybe not too much!

Appendix 1

I will make you fruitful and increase your numbers. I will make
you an assembly of peoples, and I will give this land to your
seed as an everlasting possession. (Genesis 48.4)

There are three promises here. The first is that God would *make Jacob
fruitful and increase his numbers*. The fulfilment of that promise has
already been noted, just a few verses previously – Genesis 47.27 says
'Thus Israel settled in the land of Egypt, in the region of Goshen;
and they gained possessions in it, *and were fruitful and multiplied
exceedingly*' (the Hebrew in the two places is the same). The second promise, which refers to making Jacob a *company of peoples*, is
just about to be fulfilled. Jacob is just about to claim Joseph's sons
Manasseh and Ephraim as his own (in Gen. 48.5), thereby complet-
ing the list of the 12 tribes, in which each tribe bears the name of one
of Joseph's brothers or one of his two sons. One of the reasons that
Jacob's reference to this second promise is interesting is that when
God made it, at Luz, in Genesis 35, God used the phrase 'company of
nations'. The phrase 'company of *peoples*' comes from Isaac's blessing
of Jacob in Gen 28.3, before he went to Luz. Strictly speaking, Jacob
doesn't ever become a company of nations (that is more true of Abraham than of Jacob). However, 'company of peoples' refers perfectly
to the 12 tribes that Jacob becomes when he claims Joseph's two sons
as his own in Genesis 48.5. So here is a second promise fulfilled.
The third promise is a promise of land as a 'perpetual holding'. This
language is never used by God in a promise to Jacob, but it is used
in God's promise to Abraham in Genesis 17.8, 'And I will give to
you, and to your offspring after you, the land where you are now an
alien, all the land of Canaan, for a perpetual holding; and I will be

their God.' Even though God never uses the language of perpetual holding in a promise to Jacob, two brief passages confirm for the reader that the promise was fulfilled for both Abraham and Isaac. In Genesis 28.4 (the verse immediately after the verse in which Isaac uses the language of 'company of peoples'), Isaac says to Jacob 'May he give to you the blessing of Abraham, to you and to your offspring with you, so that you may take possession of the land where you now live as an alien – land that God gave to Abraham.' (Note the past tense.) In Genesis 35.12, similarly, we read, 'The land that I gave to Abraham and Isaac I will give to you, and I will give the land to your offspring after you'.

That has been a lot of technical detail! Let me throw just one more piece in before I say something about what it all means, and why it is important in terms of thinking about resilience. I talked above about the special phrases in Genesis 47.29 ('put your hand under my thigh' and 'promise to deal loyally and truly with me') and their links with Genesis 24, the story of Abraham's commission to his servant to find a wife for Isaac, and not to get him a wife from among the Canaanite women. Both Genesis 24 and Genesis 28 involve ancestors taking steps to find a wife for the 'chosen' son, and both stress the importance of choosing a Terahite (i.e. from the family of Abraham's father, Terah) and not a Canaanite girl. I'm pointing that out not in order to stress the 'not a Canaanite' bit (even though Joseph's wife is Egyptian and not a Terahite), but rather to point out the very tight network of texts and promises that Jacob's statement of God's promise to him in Genesis 48.3–4 draws together. Genesis 17.8; 24.2, 9 and 49; 28.3–4; and 48.3–4 share multiple common themes and language, and the linking of these texts builds a kind of framework of divine promises to Abraham, Isaac and Jacob across Genesis. And, as I've already suggested, when they're all put together, they suggest that the promises have already been fulfilled. (I'll say some more about why I think that's true of the land promise in the main body of the chapter.)

Appendix 2

Do you remember I said above that Sarah has Hagar and Ishmael sent away so that Ishmael won't inherit along with Isaac? That is another story of two mothers, in which the firstborn is not the son of the preferred wife. Abraham doesn't follow Deuteronomy 21.17 either (in fact, he doesn't give Ishmael or his other sons by Keturah anything at all by way of inheritance, although he gives gifts to the sons of his concubines [Gen 25.1–6]). We don't see language in Genesis 21 that alludes strongly to Deuteronomy 21.17 as we do in Jacob's case, but there is an intriguing inversion of the Jacob story. In Genesis 21 Abraham breaches Deuteronomy 21.17 and sends away his Egyptian son without an inheritance. In Genesis 48 Jacob breaches Deuteronomy 21.17 and gives a *double inheritance* to his Egyptian son!

Do you remember that in Chapter Two I talked about the interpretation of Mrs Potiphar's seduction attempt that took seriously the idea that Potiphar is described as a eunuch – and raised the possibility that the Potiphars were working in league to get a son for themselves by Joseph? If you liked that interpretation, you might have noticed a second inversion between the stories of Isaac and of Joseph: Sarah and Abraham are Israelites who co-opt their Egyptian slave as surrogate, while the Potiphars are Egyptians who co-opt their Israelite slave to help get them a child! The two inversions of the Isaac story in the Joseph story suggest not only a relationship between the two stories, but also that there might be some underlying political point being made about ethnicity in them.

There is something else very mysterious about Joseph's inheritance: the phrase 'the portion that I took from the hand of the Amorites with my sword and with my bow'. 'Why is that mysterious?' you might ask. Well, first, there is no story anywhere in Genesis about Jacob taking anything from the Amorites, or indeed anybody else, with sword or bow. Jacob tends more toward peacefulness. Second, the Hebrew word that Jacob uses to mean portion here, *shekem*, is a play on the name of the town 'Shechem', in which Joseph's brothers Simeon and Levi slaughter all the males, plundering their wealth, following the sexual assault on Dinah (Genesis 34). Notably, in that story Jacob disapproves of his sons' extreme violence, preferring a more eirenic response to the attack on his daughter. So why the unnecessary, and inaccurate, reference to Jacob's war-making?

There are two possibilities. One is that the author wanted to draw the reader's attention to the violence of Simeon and Levi, because it is the reason they are about to be passed over in terms of blessing in Chapter 49. The second is that the author may have wanted to allude to the two very different approaches to possession of land that I talked about in Chapter Six. Simeon and Levi represent the approach in which the owner must dispossess the former occupants of the land, with violence if necessary. Jacob represents the approach in which the owner of land lives alongside others also in the land, doing their best to resolve conflict through peaceable means. And perhaps the authors wanted to do this just at the point when Jacob is about to bless the very 12 tribes who will go on to inherit the promised land by violent conquest.

So, Joseph gets the firstborn's inheritance of a double portion, but he gets it in a manner that suggests that perhaps it's not really about him at all, but instead is about other things like ethnicity or land.

Appendix 3

Jacob's blessings of his 12 sons do not always fit the pattern of the story terribly well. However, in some parts they match the story very well, and we see a great example in the observation in Genesis 49.26 that Joseph had been set apart from his brothers. There is an interesting twist here, however. There is no verb with the sense 'to set apart' in the final phrase of Jacob's blessing of Joseph – the sense of being 'set apart' is instead conveyed by a noun. The noun is 'nazirite'. A nazirite was a man who was given (usually while still young) a special relationship with God. Nazirites were not only set apart *from* other people, but set apart *to* God (Numbers 6). The best example of a nazirite is Samuel. When Samuel's mother was unable to conceive, she prayed to God, making God a vow that if God would give her a male child she would set him before God as a nazirite (1 Sam. 1.11). Samson was also a nazirite, but he was promised by God to his mother as a nazirite before his birth (Judges 13). So, after all of Joseph's pious language, here is Jacob saying that Joseph really was a man of God all along (of course, Jacob was always biased!) If Joseph has been sidelined from leadership of his people so that Judah is the 'king' and not he, then Joseph is apparently established, by Jacob's blessing, as a man of God in the manner of the judges.

Further Reading

N.B. Those items marked '*' are highly accessible and particularly suitable for readers with little or no background. Unmarked items are accessible to all readers. Those marked '**' are more academic in nature.

General – Trauma

*Haines, Steve. *Trauma is Really Strange*. Jessica Kingsley: London, 2016.

Kraus, Laurie, David Holyan and Bruce Wismer. *Recovering from Un-Natural Disasters*. Louisville, KY: Westminster John Knox, 2017.

Levine, Peter A. *In an Unspoken Voice: How the Body Releases Trauma and Restores Goodness*. Berkeley: North Atlantic, 2010.

Van der Kolk, Bessel. *The Body Keeps the Score: Brain, Mind and Body in the Healing of Trauma*. New York: Penguin, 2015.

Warner, Megan, Christopher Southgate, Carla Grosch-Miller and Hilary Ison. *Tragedies and Christian Congregations: The Practical Theology of Trauma*. London: Routledge, 2020.

157

General – Resilience

*American Psychological Association,

'The Road to Resilience: What is Resilience?' <www.apa.org/helpcenter/road-resilience.aspx>

Birkett, Kirsten. *Resilience: A Spiritual Project*. Latimer Studies 84; London: Latimer Trust, 2015.

**Randall, William L. 'The Importance of Being Ironic: Narrative Openness and Personal Resilience in Later Life', *The Gerontologist* 53 (2013): 9–16.

Whitehead, James D. and Evelyn Eaton Whitehead.
The Virtue of Resilience. Maryknoll, NY: Orbis, 2016.

General – Trauma, Resilience and the Bible

**Boase, Elizabeth and Christopher Frechette, eds.
Bible through the Lens of Trauma. Semeia Studies 86; Atlanta: SBL, 2016.

Carr, David M. *Holy Resilience: The Bible's Traumatic Origins*. New Haven: Yale University, 2014.

General – Trauma, Resilience and Theology

Jones, Serene. *Trauma and Grace*. New York: Westminster, 2009.

**Rambo, Shelly. *Spirit and Trauma: A Theology of Remaining*. Louisville, KY: Westminster John Knox, 2010.

**Southgate, Christopher.	*Theology in a Suffering World: Glory and Longing.* Cambridge: Cambridge University, 2018.
Swinton, John.	*Raging with Compassion: Pastoral Responses to the Problem of Evil.* Grand Rapids, MI/Cambridge: Eerdmans, 2007.

Genesis

**Brett, Mark, G.	*Genesis: Identity and the Politics of Procreation.* (London: Routledge, 2000).
*Warner, Megan	*Abraham: A Journey through Lent.* London: SPCK, 2015.
**Warner, Megan.	*Re-Imagining Abraham: A Re-Assessment of the Influence of Deuteronomism in Genesis.* OTS 72; Leiden/Boston: Brill, 2018.

Chapter Two

Garner, Helen	*The First Stone: Some Questions about Sex and Power* (Melbourne: Picador Australia, 1995).
Herman, Judith.	*Trauma and Recovery: The Aftermath of Violence (from domestic abuse to political terror).* New York: Basic, 1997.

Chapter Three

**Ganzevoort, R. Ruard.	'Religious Coping Reconsidered, Part Two: A Narrative Reformulation'. *Journal of Psychology and Theology* 26, no. 3 (1998): 276–286.

Levinson, Bernard M.   *Legal Revision and Religious Renewal in Ancient Israel.* New York: Cambridge University, 2008.

Goleman, Larry A. (ed.).   *Finding our Story: Narrative Leadership and Congregational Change.* Lanham, MD: Rowman and Littlefield, 2010.

Chapter Five

**Brett, Mark G.   *Political Trauma and Healing: Biblical Ethics for a Postcolonial World.* Grand Rapids: Eerdmans, 2016.

*Frankl, Viktor E.   *Man's Search for Meaning.* New York: Washington Square, 1985.

**Volkan, Vamik D.   *Bloodlines: From Ethnic Pride to Ethnic Terrorism.* New York: Farrar, Straus and Giroux, 1997.

An easy way to get to know the Bible

'For those who've been putting aside two years in later life to read the Bible from cover to cover, the good news is: the most important bits are here.' Jeremy Vine, BBC Radio 2

The Bible is full of dramatic stories that have made it the world's bestselling book. But whoever has time to read it all from cover to cover? Now here's a way of getting to know the Bible without having to read every chapter and verse.

No summary, no paraphrase, no commentary: just the Bible's own story in the Bible's own words.

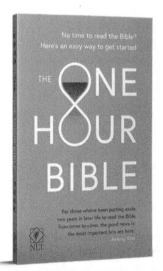

'What an amazing concept! This compelling, concise, slimmed-down Scripture is a must for anyone who finds those sixty-six books a tad daunting.'
Paul Kerensa, comedian and script writer

'A great introduction to the main stories in the Bible and it helps you to see how they fit together. It would be great to give as a gift.'
Five-star review on Amazon

The One Hour Bible
978 0 281 07964 3 • £4.99

WE HAVE A VISION OF A WORLD IN WHICH EVERYONE IS TRANSFORMED BY CHRISTIAN KNOWLEDGE

As well as being an award-winning publisher, SPCK is the oldest Anglican mission agency in the world.

Our mission is to lead the way in creating books and resources that help everyone to make sense of faith.

Will you partner with us to put good books into the hands of prisoners, great assemblies in front of schoolchildren and reach out to people who have not yet been touched by the Christian faith?

To donate, please visit www.spckpublishing.co.uk/donate or call our friendly fundraising team on 020 7592 3900.